FRIENDSHIP

PASTORING FOR LIFE

Theological Wisdom for Ministering Well

Jason Byassee, Series Editor

Aging: Growing Old in Church
by Will Willimon

Friendship: The Heart of Being Human
by Victor Lee Austin

*Recovering: From Brokenness and Addiction to
Blessedness and Community*
by Aaron White

Other Books by Victor Lee Austin

A Priest's Journal

Up with Authority

Priest in New York

Christian Ethics: A Guide for the Perplexed

Losing Susan

FRIENDSHIP

THE HEART OF

BEING HUMAN

VICTOR LEE AUSTIN

Baker Academic

a division of Baker Publishing Group

Grand Rapids, Michigan

Published by Baker Academic
a division of Baker Publishing Group
PO Box 6287, Grand Rapids, MI 49516-6287
www.bakeracademic.com

Printed in the United States of America

Library of Congress Cataloging-in-Publication Data
Names: Austin, Victor Lee, 1956– author.
Title: Friendship : the heart of being human / Victor Lee Austin.
Description: Grand Rapids, Michigan : Baker Academic, a division of Baker Publishing Group, 2020. | Series: Pastoring for life: theological wisdom for ministering well | Includes index.
Identifiers: LCCN 2019048619 | ISBN 9781540960849 (paperback)
Subjects: LCSH: Friendship—Religious aspects—Christianity. | Theological anthropology—Christianity. | Pastoral theology.
Classification: LCC BV4647.F7 A97 2020 | DDC 241/.6762—dc23
LC record available at https://lccn.loc.gov/2019048619

ISBN: 978-1-5409-6317-8 (casebound)

20   21   22   23   24   25   26   7   6   5   4   3   2   1

To my friends
and Friend

Contents

Series Preface

One of the great privileges of being a pastor is that people seek out your presence in some of life's most jarring transitions. They want to give thanks. Or cry out for help. They seek wisdom and think you may know where to find some. Above all, they long for God, even if they wouldn't know to put it that way. I remember phone calls that came in a rush of excitement, terror, and hope. "We had our baby!" "It looks like she is going to die." "I think I'm going to retire." "He's turning sixteen!" "We got our diagnosis." Sometimes the caller didn't know why they were calling their pastor. They just knew it was a good thing to do. They were right. I will always treasure the privilege of being in the room for some of life's most intense moments.

And, of course, we don't pastor only during intense times. No one can live at that decibel level all the time. We pastor in the ordinary, the mundane, the beautiful (or depressing!) day-by-day most of the time. Yet it is striking how often during those everyday moments our talk turns to the transitions of birth, death, illness, and the beginning and end of vocation. Pastors sometimes joke, or lament, that we are only ever called when people want to be "hatched, matched, or dispatched"—born or baptized, married, or eulogized. But those are moments we share with all humanity, and they are good moments in which to do gospel work. As an American, it feels perfectly natural to ask a couple how they met. But a South African friend told me he feels this is exceedingly intrusive! What I am really asking is how someone met God as they met the person to whom they have made lifelong promises. I am asking about transition and encounter—the tender places where the God of cross and resurrection meets us. And I am thinking about how to bear witness amid the transitions that are our lives. Pastors are the ones who get phone calls at these moments and have the joy, burden, or just plain old workaday job of showing up with oil for anointing, with prayers, to be a sign of the Holy Spirit's overshadowing goodness in all of our lives.

I am so proud of this series of books. The authors are remarkable, the scholarship first-rate, the prose readable—even elegant—the claims made ambitious and then well defended. I am especially pleased because so often in the church we play small ball. We argue with one another over intramural matters while the world around us struggles, burns, ignores, or otherwise proceeds on its way. The problem is that the gospel of Jesus Christ isn't just for the renewal of the church. It's for the renewal of the cosmos—everything God bothered to create in the first place. God's gifts are not *for* God's people. They are *through* God's people, *for* everybody else. These authors write with wisdom, precision, insight, grace, and good humor. I so love the books that have resulted. May God use them to bring glory to God's name, grace to God's children, renewal to the church, and blessings to the world that God so loves and is dying to save.

Jason Byassee

Invocation

Many pastoral situations involve change: a new life or a life passing away; the arrival of a new love or the loss of love; the launch of a new job and career or the dwindling of powers and opportunities, being laid off, laid aside, passed over. As the Preacher said, "A time to be born, and a time to die; a time to plant, and a time to pluck up that which is planted; . . . a time to weep, and a time to laugh; a time to mourn, and a time to dance; a time to cast away stones, and a time to gather stones together; a time to embrace, and a time to refrain from embracing" (Eccles. 3:2–5). Wisdom recognizes that human life is full of transitions. What remains constant? What endures?

This book about friendship is about something that lasts. You can lose your job, but that need not make you less human. You can lose your spouse, your bank account, your country, your digital identity, your health. None of these losses need diminish your humanity. Because through every transition of life, friendship is the heart of who you are.

Friendship is why we exist in the first place. Friendship is also our final end in the kingdom of God. Out of friendship God has made us, for friendship he has died for us, to friendship he ever draws us.

Let us pray. *Dear Lord Jesus, only Son of the Father, we entrust unto thee all who read this book, that thy Holy Spirit would preserve in their heart whatever is true herein and drive from remembrance anything that may be false. In every transition of our life, we, children of dust, place our trust in thee: our never-failing, ever-merciful, tender, and firm to the end Maker, Defender, Redeemer, and Friend.*[1]

Introduction

An Invitation to Friendship

The Background to This Book: The Death of Susan

Susan and I had married right after college, in a traditional Episcopal Church ceremony of "holy matrimony," promising therein to have and to hold in sickness and in health "till death us do part." I had loved her from the first time I heard her talk, which was in a Bible study at the decidedly secular St. John's College in Santa Fe, New Mexico. It was fifteen years into our marriage when her brain tumor was found. The medical professionals successfully treated it—first with surgery and then, when the biopsy showed that her astrocytoma had a mid-grade malignancy, with radiation and chemotherapy. Her cancer never returned. But the treatments weakened her brain in ways that, although slow to manifest themselves, proved inexorable. She needed more sleep; she lost the capacity to initiate tasks and carry them through; she grew quieter as she found it harder to locate the words she wanted to say. These were some of the manifestations of her brain disease, which, although it took nineteen years, in the end took her life.

I had longed for Susan to love me and for me to be able to love her. In giving her to me, God, true to his promise, had given me what I most desired. So does one read in, for instance, Psalm 37:4, "Take delight in the LORD, and he shall give you your heart's desire."[1] Yet I believe it is necessary to say that God also took my heart's desire

1

away. I don't mean that at a particular moment (a Monday in late Advent, about 9 a.m. eastern standard time) God looked down from his seat in a distant heavenly abode and said, "I'm going to take Susan away from Victor and bring her home to me." Such a view of God is crude and nonsensical. God is not in any place. And he is not in time. Which is to say, he is not an actor within the universe. God is not like the president of the United States, who could indeed say that he is going to remove his ambassador from Austria and bring her home to Washington. He is not like the CEO of IBM, who could say that she is going to close down operations in Houston and lay off workers there and leave them to their own devices to find other jobs. (Dear readers in Houston, this is a hypothetical. I write these words having no idea whether IBM has ever had operations in your fair city.) And God is not like the head honcho of a smuggling operation, who could decide that a particular individual is no longer of use but unfortunately knows too much to remain at large and therefore must be terminated.

No, God did not take Susan away in a fashion comparable to any possible action of an in-the-world actor. Rather, it is as the one responsible for the world being a world in the first place that he took her away. The world that exists—the world that God is responsible for—is, as Antoine de Saint-Exupéry's little prince learns, ephemeral. Its character is marked throughout by transience, by loss. Susan has died; the flowers of last Easter have withered; the ancient mountains have been covered by the sea; you, dear reader, will one day yourself die and fade away like the grass and be covered over by all that follows you. This is the world. This is all God's work. For all this, both giving and taking, God is responsible. As Job perceived, "Naked came I out of my mother's womb, and naked shall I return thither: the LORD gave, and the LORD hath taken away" (1:21). Not as president, not as CEO, not as boss, but as the strange creator: God is responsible. It is that strangeness that drives Job to continue the verse saying, nevertheless, "Blessed be the name of the LORD."

So I was married to my heart's desire. As I begin writing this book some years after Susan's death, I find that I am no longer sad about her dying, nor am I angry with God. I do not deny that sad-like feelings may surface when, for instance, I come across photos of her with me in the early days of our marriage. On my mother's desk, I see one that makes me wistful: Susan looks up with beauty and intelligence; it is just past her twenty-fifth birthday; she is holding our firstborn child. I pause before such a picture and know what time and disease will do; I see promise that I know will not be fulfilled. But today there is something else to see, something far from wistfulness and regret, something more important. It is the love of God, right there in the picture. It simply is the case that everything God gives us is finite and just so will have an end. But that the gift has an end does not take away the fact that it was a gift and that it was good, which is why Job does not say only "The LORD gave, and the LORD hath taken away" but also "Blessed be the name of the LORD."

A couple of years after Susan died, I happened to be on a retreat, compliments of the far-seeing people of the Church Pension Fund who seek to encourage clergy wellness. This clergy retreat had talks and exercises on finances and spiritual practices and physical and psychological health. It surrounded these talks with prayer. So there we were, one day, in a "healing Eucharist." Now I hope, patient reader, that it won't stop you from going on in this book to learn that I have voiced curmudgeonly views about prayers for healing being made part of the Eucharist. I do not like them. It seems to me that people often get in line for such prayers without any illness in particular that they wish to have God heal. It is sheer superstition (the curmudgeon says) to ask for the laying on of hands and anointing with oil for healing when one doesn't have something in particular to ask for. (I also have doubts about being anointed on behalf of someone else—after all, you can't be baptized for someone else, or receive Communion for someone else, or get married or ordained for someone else. But that's another sermon for another day.) Too many people, this curmudgeon says judgmentally, get anointed in these healing services for fear that they might have some unknown illness. They fear that if they aren't anointed, God will let the hypothetical illness get them. That is superstition.

So I am sitting there, judgmentally, indeed self-righteously ("God, I thank thee that I am not like these other people, who get anointed out of sheer superstition"), when it comes to me that I have never asked to be healed from Susan's death.

Chastened, I get up and shuffle into line.

When my time comes, I tell the two people who are there to pray for me that (as they already know) my wife has died and (what they don't know) I have never asked to be healed from that loss. They put their hands on me, and after a bit of silence, one of them begins. "Lord, we thank you that you have given Victor something that many people never get to experience." The tears flow freely from my eyes, for instantly I interpret her as saying, "God gave you a long marriage, which many people desire but do not have"—and I get it.

I can see now that it is good to thank God for everything, including evils like disease. As the Book of Common Prayer has put it—in words that go back to 1549, words that Susan and I heard as we grew closer together, kneeling or standing side by side—"It is very meet, right, and our bounden duty, that we should at all times, and in all places, give thanks unto thee."[2] "At all times and in all places" includes the hospital bedside and the grave. But what I heard in that prayer for my healing did not have to do with Susan's long illness or her more recent death. I heard thanks being given for the marriage itself. It was held out there for me to see as if for the first time: God's great gift to me of Susan for thirty-four years. Many people yearn for marriage but never receive it or, being married, find it ends after a short time. That our marriage had come to an end did not cause it to cease being a true gift of God. Although God had taken Susan away, it was still true that he had given her to me in the first place—and for an amazing stretch of more than a third of a century.

In those days I was theologian-in-residence of Saint Thomas Church Fifth Avenue in New York City. Suddenly one summer our world-class organist, John Scott, died. We all felt he was too young to die; he was truly at the peak of his powers, renowned and loved especially by our congregation and the boys of our choir school. Yet now he was dead. At the end of his sermon at John's funeral, Andrew Mead, the rector who had brought John to Saint Thomas, spoke aloud the question we are often afraid to voice: "You may have asked the Lord, 'Why have you done this, taking John away like this?' For me, it has helped to widen the question: 'Lord, why did you give John to us in the first place; why was there a John Scott at all?' This provides room for gratitude within our grief. For what a privilege it is to have heard, seen, and known John Scott!"

Every gift of God is a finite gift: to be *this* gift means that it has a shape and limits. That a gift has an end does not take away its goodness. A rose is no less beautiful because it will fade; the lovely skin of a baby is no less lovely to us who know of future acne, weathering, and scarring; a painting loses none of its interest even though it terminates at the frame. Indeed, it is built into the very idea of a material creation that it be finite. Any thing whatsoever is a *this* and not a *that*, *here* and not *there*; it exists at one time—and not at another.

I grieved Susan's brain disease, her diminishments, and finally her death. Yet she would have died at some time nonetheless, for every human life is finite. And every marriage is finite. It begins with vows. It ends, as plainly stated in those very vows, in the death of one or the other spouse.

There is much more to be said about God's character as one who gives and takes away, and I have tried to explore those depths in my earlier book *Losing Susan*. Here I have written these introductory words so that you will know that marriage forms the background of the book in your hands. The author before you was married and now he is not. These days he finds himself in wonderment over friendship, about what its shape is, what might be its limits. He wants to have friends, indeed good friends, and hopes that somehow God might be a friend also. And behind all this wondering, he has a wee bit of worry (as you will come to see) that perhaps marriage has been too much in the forefront of our churches' thinking, that perhaps in the life of our churches we need to move marriage a bit to the background and try for a while to foreground friendship.

For there is a signal difference between marriage and friendship. Although marriage might be a kind of friendship or might have a partial overlap with friendship (we will need to explore this), nonetheless friendship is clearly a different thing. One needs only to note the irreducible fact that friendship has no vows term-limited by death.

Will You Come with Me?

This book, then, is not an academic treatise but a journey into friendship, a quest prompted by a question. I start with perplexity about what friendship is and a hunch that it is more important than anything else. I have also a sense that our culture has lost something, that there is a hole in our reality where friendship needs to be. In the presence of such perplexity, what shall we do? It won't do to try to have friends if we don't know what friends are or why we need them. The way forward is, in part, the way back. I will go first to the ancients, some pre-Christian thinkers of the West. My approach to classic writings is to skip over middle management (e.g., commentators and textbooks) and go straight to the source.[3] If you come with me, we will dig into a few key sections of Aristotle—whose teaching about friendship, although immeasurably influential, ends tragically. We will turn to a short Platonic dialogue that is generally thought to be unsuccessful but which, I believe, actually shows the achievement of the beginning of friendship. And we will enjoy Cicero's elegant prose, even though he shares Aristotle's tragic elements.

But we will do all this probing of ancient wisdom as people who bear the scriptural narrative. The Bible itself can be seen as a text that is a journey into friendship (it will keep appearing throughout the book in your hands). We also need to take account of Augustine, the first Christian who gives a theology of friendship, and Aquinas, who has some breathtaking things to say about it. A hero of our journey will be Aelred of Rievaulx, a monk of the twelfth century who despite having had little time to write manages to point out ways to solve the Aristotelian/Ciceronian conundrum—to turn tragedy into good news.

Once we come to see how supremely important friendship is for our flourishing as human beings—and its centrality to our salvation—then we will want to ask further questions about our culture, not only in critique but also with an eye to finding hints of ways to practice friendship anew. For although this book is a journey in thought, it has in the end existential urgency. We just won't be able to be really human if we do not have real friends.

ONE

The Limits of Marriage

The Problematic Fallout of Marriage Debates

Why would we look for friendship? It might seem that our heart's desire is for intimacy and companionship, to have another who will know us and whom we will know, within an embrace of love and truth. But isn't that what marriage is?

Contemporary controversies over marriage in Western societies and churches go back a good century. Before there were questions about same-sex relationships, there were questions about the place of children in marriage (whether technology can permissibly shape procreation and, if so, how, starting with questions about contraception). Then not that far in the past, questions arose about remarriage after divorce. Views on all sides of these matters have been passionately held, calling forth a lot of thinking and debating, as they should. Developments in society have been seen by some church folk as revelations of new things that God is doing in the world; accordingly, they have urged their churches to reform what they viewed as outdated practices. But others, instead, have found those same societal developments to be temptations to deviate from the truth, and they have urged faithful resistance. And still others have wanted to hold on to traditional beliefs but have felt that pastoral concerns require some measure of accommodation.

What is common to these controversies is that each has led to calls that the shape of marriage be changed and that the limits placed upon marriage be relaxed. There has been a resulting counter-response that urges a defense of marriage, which, it is said, is under attack and has been so for some time. As a result, the energies of the churches have been concentrated on the marital institution to such an extent that, arguably, we have failed to attend to other important things, including friendship.

Perhaps today we need to set aside for a while our disputes over marriage and bring friendship to the fore.

Jesus and the Nonresurrection of Marriage

It is built into the marriage vow that it exists only for this life. While everything that belongs to creation is finite and has limits, it is peculiar to marriage that those limits are expressly this-worldly. Forgive me if I belabor the point; it is, it seems to me, signally unappreciated by Christians in general. In the kingdom of heaven there are human beings, free of sin and doing such great things as humans have the capacity to do. They are fully human—and they do not marry. Marriage is the only social institution that Jesus identifies as not part of human flourishing in the kingdom of his Father.

When some opponents wanted to trap Jesus, they concocted (or co-opted) a scenario according to which a woman had had seven husbands, all of them brothers, each of them taking up with her, as the Mosaic law required, after his predecessor had, well, expired (in each case leaving her childless). These opponents (they were the Sadducees) believed this scenario exposed a problem with holding that there is a resurrection (a doctrine they rejected): if dead people are raised, then this woman, when she is raised, will have seven husbands! Jesus' refutation is clean and simple: in the resurrection there is no marriage. Here is how Saint Luke records his reply: "The children of this world marry, and are given in marriage: But they which shall be accounted worthy to obtain that world, and the resurrection from the dead, neither marry, nor are given in marriage: Neither can they die any more: for they are equal unto the angels; and are the children of God, being the children of the resurrection" (Luke 20:34–36). It is briefer in Saint Matthew: "For in the resurrection they neither marry, nor are given in marriage, but are as the angels of God in heaven" (Matt. 22:30). Similarly brief, Saint Mark still gets in a reference to the dead: "For when they shall rise from the dead, they neither marry, nor are given in marriage; but are as the angels which are in heaven" (Mark 12:25).

The main point of this encounter is Jesus' affirmation that there is such a thing as "the resurrection" or a rising "from the dead," over against the Sadducees' teaching that denied it. Since it seems they also denied the existence of angels, Jesus' claim that in the resurrection humans are "equal unto" or "as the angels" is a further underscoring of their difference. To avoid misunderstanding, we should note that Jesus merely compares the resurrected human life with the angelic, and only on this point: just as angels do not marry (nor do they die), so for people in the resurrection. He does not say, for instance, that in the resurrection people are like angels in having no bodies; he does not characterize the resurrection as an ongoing eternal life of a disembodied soul. Most emphatically, he does not say that we die as women and men but rise as angels. It is human beings who "shall rise from the dead," and they shall not marry.

This is no minor aspect of our Lord's teaching. Rather, it is his key illustration of both the real promise of the resurrection and the real difference between this life and that one: there is marriage now, and there will not be marriage then. Marriage is temporally circumscribed; it is this-worldly; it is not a part of the life to come. Every marriage has a beginning and has, or will have, an end. To reject this reality is to indulge in fantasy and set oneself up for failure. I recall one of the first couples I prepared for marriage. During our premarital conversations, the groom-to-be balked at the words in the wedding vow "until we are parted by death." Words that reference death, he felt, would be a downer; they would throw a shadow on what should be an exceedingly happy day. This groom wanted, instead of the vow as written, to say that his love would last forever. Green priest as I then was, I am sure I did not help him much. Yet alas, as it turned out, they were soon divorced; far short of forever, their marriage did not last even a few years. Reality can be hard, but fantasy can be worse.

Is There Something We're Not Seeing?

O Christians! Do you want to be saying that the highest, most important achievement for a human being is marriage, when it is clear from Scripture and liturgy (if not from popular human sentiment) that marriage is for this world only? Does it make for a truly coherent Christian doctrine of the human being to say that what is most important this side of death does not even exist on the other side? For (as we dare not forget) "on the other side" we will still be human beings, we will still have bodies—indeed, Christians affirm Jesus' bodily ascension into heaven—and yet, in the resurrection, there is not to be marriage. Respect for our created nature cannot require us taking marriage as the highest thing.

Is there something else on offer, something we should cease overlooking and bring to the center of our attention, at least for a while?

There is, and that something else is, of course, friendship. Let me propose an answer to a question implicit a few pages back. If we are fully human in the life to come, what is the characteristic human activity of that life? This is my answer, which I first heard suggested by Herbert McCabe, a brilliant thinker of the last century: heaven is people living together as friends—friends with each other, friends with God.[1]

The characteristic activity of a human being is to live in friendship with others.

The rest of this book will try to bring light to this conclusion. We will learn from philosophy, the Bible, Christian thinkers, literature, and indeed our own pondering over what makes sense.

To speak honestly, most of us know little about friendship. We are confused by it, and consequently we don't know how to work on it, and thus we underprize it. It is a great puzzle. While the limits and nature of marriage are hotly contested, we muddle along in blindness to something that is arguably more universal than marriage and more eternally important.

I awoke to this reality a few years ago. Shortly after Susan died, my children, who were then independent young adults, gently and lovingly told me that they would have no objection if I wanted to remarry. Other friends occasionally asked about such things. I remember a question from a priest—"Are you seeing anyone?"—which surprised me, although it turned out he was wondering not if I had taken up a new romance but if I was seeing a psychologist to work through grief! Still, the question of seeing or dating or marrying is often there, even if not always given voice. And it's not wrong, but it is interesting that no one asked me how my friendships were doing. My immediate thoughts after Susan died turned to my calling from God. As a priest in the Episcopal Church, I could remarry as a matter of course, just as all Christian laypeople may regardless of their church. It is different for Orthodox and Roman Catholic clergy. In the Orthodox tradition, marriage, if it comes at all, must precede ordination, and a priest (male, of course) whose wife dies cannot remarry. Similar provisions apply to former Episcopal clergy who are ordained in the Roman Catholic Church, and indeed they apply to married deacons within that church itself.

Wise, practical reasons can be discerned behind such a tradition—it keeps the priest from being "on the market" among his or her parishioners; it's a boundary that protects pastoral care from turning into a romantic relationship, which could easily sour and harm people. But I felt another reason as well.

Taking care of Susan through her illness had consumed a large part of my attention for nearly two decades. That was time gladly given for the most part (albeit I was sometimes grumpy and unreasonable), and through those decades I learned a lot about myself and grew in ways I would not otherwise have grown. For me, as is the case for many, marriage proved a school in which I learned the joyous practices of sacrificial love. But when Susan died, I saw I would have a lot more time to put at God's disposal. With grown children, and without a spouse, I would be free to serve God wherever he called me.

And that is the case: I am at God's disposal, and already I have moved once in response to his call, as I discerned it, not to India (where I had a bit of a fancy he might send me) but to Dallas. (For many New Yorkers, Dallas is at a *greater* cultural remove than India.) I call myself a theological missionary, someone sent by God to teach and write to help people better understand divine and human things.

Then I thought some more. I was married immediately after college. I never had those post-college single years in which many people develop friendships while living alone. It's happening to me in reverse, it seems. I married first, and now I am in a time of life to explore what friendship is, to try to make and build friendships, and to learn to be a friend. I am a missionary into friendship, as someone who sees friendship not as a possible preliminary to marriage but as the reverse. Friendship is the good thing that extends beyond any possible marriage. What is it? Premarital, postmarital, extramarital, intramarital, nonmarital—all of these at once and, in fact, something that need not have any intrinsic connection with marriage.

It's obvious, at least from my standpoint in life, that friendship is the highest human thing. It is, may I say, the final frontier. It is the long game. But what is it?

TWO

The Confusions of Friendship

Our Cultural Landscape

It is a venerable strategy: when you are trying to grasp something that is not clear, you can begin by attending to how people use the word. *Friend*, we quickly see, is a word used in many different ways that suggest several different things. Here are some notes on our cultural landscape of friendship.

Contrary to what we might expect, many people employ the word *friend* to suggest distance rather than intimacy. One sees this at the time of a romantic breakup; the two parties might say to one another, "Let's just be friends." Thereby they reveal that they think of friendship as something vaguely cordial but lacking closeness, something that falls short of a real relationship.

Now turn to an aspect of the great cultural-shifting gift we have from Mr. Zuckerberg, whose Facebook has verbed the term *friend*, thereby debasing the friendship currency promiscuously. Of course, to "verb" a noun is part of the fun of English. It's not the verbing of *friend* that's culturally significant but the casualness of the process: "friending" someone amounts to no more than a click of a digital synapse. To say that you have, or to set out to acquire, thousands of friends wantonly cheapens the notion. This is acknowledged still, if guiltily, when one announces that one has a certain number of not "friends" but "Facebook friends." Yet "friending" continues to gallop along.

Other cases, however, point in the opposite direction, with *friend* indicating neither someone put off at a distance nor a person breezily "friended" but someone who is close and special. Spoken of in this way, a friend is a person intimate to oneself. Many people will say their spouse is their best friend, or they wish he or she were. Two people who are sexually attracted to each other will try to see if they can be best friends for each other as a sort of test before they commit to marriage. Similarly, and increasingly, they may simply remain each other's girlfriend or boyfriend—compound terms in which the friend is a spouse-like companion in a substitute-for-marriage relationship.

Behold our culture's confusion! On the one hand, the epitome of friendship is identified with marriage, which, whether formalized or not, is widely taken to be the most meaningful human relationship. Yet on the other hand, friendships are the dregs of lesser relationships—"just friends" and "Facebook friends"—dregs left for everyone else. On all hands, friendship lacks a proper distinctiveness, and it seems to be anything or nothing at all.

Who Will Teach Us about Friendship?

If Christians have not given friendship the kind of thoughtful attention marriage has received, and if when we do start to think about friendship we realize there is a wide variety of opinion about it and indeed vast confusion even in the way we speak of friends and friendship, where should we turn for guidance? Many people would turn straight to the Bible and investigate what it has to say on the subject. And the Bible does contain deep wisdom concerning friendship. But the path of this book, as I indicate in the introduction, is to attend to some worldly and ancient wisdom before going further into the Scriptures. It just is the case that Aristotle's thinking about friendship proved decisive for much Western thought that followed. In addition, there is a lacuna in Aristotle's thought that is almost perfectly explained—and overcome—by the Scriptures. That is to say, the likes of Aristotle will both help us understand friendship and help us see better the distinctively Christian way of friendship.

So, dear reader, you will find this book going back and forth between old classical texts and the Scriptures, even as it goes back and
forth between secular cultural artifacts and Christian thinking.
Let me lay my theological cards on the table. I take the Bible to
be the Word of God written for us and speaking to us. We humans
turn to the Bible with the intelligence we have, and that intelligence
is human, which is to say that, while personal, it is not individual but
cultural and social and communal. We humans never think alone but
are ever (when we think) in some sort of dialogue or conversation
with other humans, others who include both the living and the dead.
Indeed, the Bible itself speaks in an implicit dialogue with all forms of
human wisdom, wherever found; it critiques, illuminates that which
is good, and can correct that which falls short.

With each of the ancient pagan writers this book considers, we
will bear down on one key text. I could not pretend herein to give
you a complete scholarly account of these writers or to go through
the various schools of interpretation that have been popular at different times in history. Nor do I think you would find that interesting!
What is interesting—I think, for any person, whoever we are—is
to consider with care some things these ancients said that seem to
be at once true and problematic. Their ideas about friendship still
(thousands of years later) attract people who find them beautiful. Yet
at the same time, they suggest questions that trouble.

I turn then, for the rest of this chapter, to Aristotle (384–322 BC),
the Greek marine biologist (yes!) and philosopher whose thinking on
friendship decisively shaped Western culture.

The Ancient Surprise

On the matter of friendship, Aristotle makes a claim that we are
unlikely to have expected (although it will turn out to be also the
key Christian claim about friendship). Whether our contemporaries
think of friendship as a great thing or a minor good thing, whether
they esteem it highly or not, they locate friendship in the private
realm, treating it as something that supplements, at best, the public
business of life. Aristotle's view could not be more different. For
Aristotle considers friendship to be *the point of human life*. It is not

a soothing refuge from the tasks and duties that otherwise occupy us. It is not a place of escape where we can attend to private things, a break away from the pressures of life, a time to recharge our batteries before we go out again into the real world. On the contrary, according to Aristotle's teaching, *friendship is, or should be, of our entire life the central concern.*

This is manifest in his ethical teaching. Today there are famously interminable debates about ethics as a matter of making decisions. Should one aim to bring about the best outcome ("maximize human happiness"), or should one focus on inner motivation ("follow the moral law")? These debates are between competing ethical theories about the proper grounds for coming to a decision. But making decisions, Aristotle says, is not what ethics is primarily about.

On several occasions I have taught ethics to college students, having them (as is my custom) read original texts as much as possible. So in the course of things, they get to Aristotle, and there they are surprised. Aristotle has little to say about particular choices, he does not talk about issues, he does not dwell on particular decisions— rather, he emphasizes character. He expounds the excellences (the virtues) that build up good character. And he wraps it all up with an extensive account of friendship. Ethics, to my students' surprise, turns out to be about friendship; the aim of ethics is friendship—a discovery that, taken to heart, upends one's late-modern collegiate worldview. Something the students might have taken as onerous and burdensome (ethics) turns out to be tied directly to something they desire (friendship). I call this the Aristotelian surprise: ethics aims at friendship, and friendship rightfully takes up a significant proportion of our thinking about ethics.

It was a general view. Ancient Greeks and Romans esteemed friendship as the most important thing in life. What were they talking about when they talked about friendship? How did they unravel friendship's confusions (for they had them just as we do)?

Aristotle's Classical View

Aristotle writes about ethics in two major works, the *Nicomachean Ethics* and the *Eudemian Ethics*.[1] The *Nicomachean* is more famous and more studied, but recently, British philosopher Anthony Kenny has urged a reconsideration of the *Eudemian*, seeing it as being closer in thought and style to most of the rest of Aristotle's corpus. Since Aristotle's works come to us through uncertain transmission, it is nigh impossible to settle the question of the relationship of these two texts. But since most writers (including yours truly in the past) have attended to the *Nicomachean*, I will here, for the sake of a certain freshness of exposition, set forth the views as nuanced in the *Eudemian*.

Aristotle opens with our question: "What is friendship and what are its characteristics?" He surveys various views people have, with questions that will not be unfamiliar to us. Does the word *friendship* point to one thing only, or are there many things that we just happen to call by the same name? What obligations do friends have to one another? And what is the connection of friendship to ethics? To this last question he spells out an answer: ethics is a matter of "what is noble and desirable in people's characters," and it involves acting justly, treating other people fairly. Friendship has at least this connection to ethics: we will want to act justly (ethically) with our friends and not harm them. This is the particular goodness of civic friendship; Aristotle notes that "promotion of friendship is regarded as the special task of political skill." Yet all this is little more than repeating what people commonly said (1234b18, 22, 24)[2]—however rare it is today to claim that politicians should be about the promotion of friendship!

For us as for Aristotle, the truisms that pepper our speech reflect unexamined truth claims, what we can call common sense. The problem with common sense is that it easily contradicts itself. One hears, "Absence makes the heart grow fonder," but one also hears, "Out of sight, out of mind." Well, which is it? Concerning a desire for friends, some say we are seeking another "I," a person who is like me, who likes the things I like, and so forth. Others say we want an opposite in a friend. Do likes attract? Or do opposites attract? We say both (and so did Aristotle's contemporaries).

Aristotle trusts commonsense wisdom to contain some portion of truth; indeed, there usually is a reason why a cliché has become a cliché. But when we discover apparent contradictions, we need to think more deeply. Often this involves making an appropriate distinction. For instance, take the matter of whether likes or opposites attract. It seems that in friendship I do want someone who is like me: there is a good deal of sharing in friendship, and without significant commonalities, that sharing would just be too difficult. Yet it also seems that a good friend must be unlike me in some respects; otherwise we would have no point in sharing with each other. The other would already have everything I might give, and vice versa. So we need both like and unlike: my friend must be like me but cannot simply be like me.

What then about the rather different things that we refer to as friendship? The Greek word for friendship, *philia*, is used for "love" in a wide range of cases. So one might say one loves a particular glass of wine, and one loves one's cat, and one loves one's city, and one loves one's spouse, and one loves one's wine merchant, and one loves one's household musician, and one loves a noble and wise person. All of these could be called friendships; the word *friendship* is scattered abroad liberally. But that doesn't mean we ought to assume that something is *there*, something that's the same in my friendship with my beloved wine as in my friendship with my daughter or son as in my friendship (should I be so fortunate as to obtain it) with you.

Where there is verbal confusion, Aristotle wants us to seek out the primary instance. Of all the different ways we speak of the love that is friendship, which one can claim primacy over the others? Here is a first step. We are moved to love or desire something because it is *good* or looks good to us. However, experience has taught us that what is good might not also be *pleasant*. We desire pleasant things because they appear good: the sugary confection seems good to the taste even if it is not good for us in itself. Telling gossip may be pleasant even though it is unjust and thus not good. Nonetheless, for a good person, the good and the pleasant will be the same. She will not enjoy gossip, and she will enjoy sugary confections in appropriate moderation.

Now a follow-up step. Among goods, some are good *in the abstract* while others are good *for a particular person*. ("In the abstract" means roughly "in general" or "abstracting from particular circumstances.") Health is good in the abstract (it is always good), as is a balanced diet that maintains health. Medicine may be good for a particular person at a particular time, but medicine is not good in the abstract—which just means that a healthy person does not need medicine.

Medicine that is good for a particular person may not seem good to that person and may in fact be unpleasant. In particular cases in life, it is not only true that what seems pleasant may not be good for us but also true that what is good for us may be unpleasant. Nonetheless, abstracting from particular circumstances, for a good person, the pleasant and the good are always the same. Someone who has a good character enjoys exercising her virtues while hardly thinking about it as she does so.

A third distinction (after that of the good and the pleasant, and the particular and the abstract) is between what is useful and what is good in itself. When something is useful for me, it is obviously good for me. But something could well be good in itself without having any practical value for me.

Aristotle's final distinction brings this discussion home to friendship. "Just as in the case of inanimate objects [wine, medicine, etc.] we can choose and love something for each of these reasons [it's good or pleasant or useful], so, too, in the case of human beings: we love one man for his character and virtue, another because he is serviceable and useful, and a third because he is pleasant and gives us pleasure" (1236a10–15). When that love is received and returned, and when both parties are aware of this, then they have become friends.

Thus Aristotle comes to his famous conclusion that there are three kinds of friendship. Friendship is a love for another person (a love that is received and returned) for the sake of, respectively, the *pleasant*, the *useful*, and the *good in itself*. But immediately he is careful to add that there need be no single thing that all these friendships have in common. They aren't like oaks, elms, and cedars, three species of the single genus "tree." No, only the friendship whose basis is the good in itself is truly friendship—friendship in the primary sense. Although we might call relationships based on utility or pleasure "friendships," there is no necessity to do so. You may call the coworker who often helps you a friend, but it need not be a real friendship. The same is true of the person whose company pleases you. Relationships that are useful or pleasant are often called friendships, but they might not be friendships in the primary sense.

But what does it mean to say that real friendship is based on the good?

The Pleasantest Thing for Human Beings

In the midst of making these distinctions, Aristotle states categorically, "For a human being the pleasantest thing is another human being" (1237a28). This strikes me as arrestingly true; as soon as I heard it, I knew I wouldn't forget it. Beyond the pleasure of a glass of wine, beyond the pleasure of reading a book (even a book on friendship!), maybe even beyond the contemplation of eternal truths, the pleasure we can take in being with another human being is the greatest of pleasures. All good things are better when shared with someone, and that "someone" is pleasanter than any of them.

This is true—and perhaps it is strictly true only—when that "someone" is a friend in the primary sense. Such friends, Aristotle says, will be purely good people, complete—at least in the sense that they will not need each other to be useful to them. Nonetheless, there will be pleasure in their relationship, the pleasure that good people take in sharing the goodness of each other. To quote Aristotle again, "For a human being the pleasantest thing is another human being."

Friendship—henceforth I will say simply "friend" or "friendship" when meaning this primary sense—is an activity as much as it is a state. As an activity, it "is the mutual, pleasurable choice that two people make of each other's company," and since it is founded on virtue, that choice "is nothing other than the reciprocal choice of the things that are good and pleasant in the abstract, and it is the state that finds expression in such a choice" (1237a31–34). I take Aristotle to mean that when I choose a friend who is good, I make the choice not for any usefulness we might have for each other. Together we will choose things good and pleasant in themselves and not for any particular good they may provide for us.

What do friends do? They treat "the loved one as beloved." A friend loves his friend just as a friend. If I love a friend because he is a musician, I am loving him for the music he plays, perhaps for me. If I love him because he is a doctor, that too is a movement away from the good "in the abstract" to some particular good—in this instance, healing. Aristotle draws us to that deep place of loving the loved one, just so, as beloved simply because he is my friend. Similarly, the pleasure that is derived in friendship is properly the pleasure "from the friend himself in himself; for he is loved for himself and not for being someone else" (1237b1–4). A true friendship is stable, enduring through time and events, good and bad. This stability demands the friends' mutual trust, and it takes time to build trust. A would-be friend should be tried and tested; initially indeed one has only would-be friends. (This is one reason that bad people can't have real friends: they cannot trust one another.) Thus Aristotle would come down against Facebook and also against contemporary sentimentality that thinks everyone could just be friends. There is much more to befriending than "friending." It simply is not possible to have a large number of friends; "it is difficult to make a trial of many people: you would have to go and live with each of them." Friendship is more than shopping: "Choosing a friend should not be like choosing a cloak" (1237b35–37).

Yet still, one would think that the number of virtuous people who could make good friends is a rather large number. But we are finite beings. One cannot know, prior to taking the time, whether trust can be built with a would-be friend, which means, it seems, that one is unable to know in advance who is a truly virtuous person. Furthermore, given that there are many virtuous people in the world while I am finite, I might be able to build trust with and treat as beloved only a few.

Whenever a true friendship is established, there will be a stability that undergirds happiness. A true friend does not disappear in hard times. On the contrary, in misfortune "it becomes clear that the property of friends is common." As soon as the beloved falls into need, the friend will treat her own goods (and, we could add, her time, and whatever else might be hers) as belonging not just to herself but to her friend as well. Which is to say, even when life is unstable, a true friendship maintains its stability (1238a17).

So in the end, must friends be equals? Aristotle notes many friendships that exist between unequals, and while they sometimes seem to be based on utility and pleasure, they also can be based on the good. Friendships can arise between benefactor and beneficiary, ruler and ruled, parent and child, and so forth. (One regrets to note, however unsurprising it is, that Aristotle considers the husband-wife friendship to be one of these unequal friendships; see 1238b24.) Still, the

inequality built into these friendships keeps them from being friendships in the primary sense, even if they are based on the good, for the
inequality of the parties makes their reciprocity unequal. The love
of parent and child, for instance, resembles true friendship since it is
based on the good (and not on the pleasure a parent gets from having
a child, or the usefulness a child gets from having a parent, and so
forth). But it would be wrong for a parent, holding nothing back, to
share her whole mind with her child. Such openness, which indeed is
proper to friendship, demands an equality between the friends that
is absent between parent and child; thus "it is only equal partners
that are friends" (1239a4).[3]

Now we have a complete and, many have found, attractive picture
from Aristotle of what a friendship truly is: a reciprocal love between
two virtuous people who are fundamentally equal that is based in
their human goodness and not in their usefulness to each other or
in their pleasantness to each other. Such a friendship, deeply satisfying, is uncommon but not necessarily unique; one person can have a
(small) number of friends. And such a friendship will be stable over
time and provide true happiness, true human fulfillment.

Yet this picture has its problems. It seems tragic that friendship
must be so rare an occurrence and limited to so few. A Christian could
wonder, in addition, about the absence of a dynamic of repentance
and how that might change our understanding of what is humanly
good. Such questions Aristotle does not raise. But he does raise, in
the *Eudemian Ethics*, two significant questions with implications
for theology. He asks first if, according to this picture, a man can be
friends with himself. This odd question arises if we think of a good
human being as someone who is self-sufficient. And it leads to an
even odder question: Why does God have no friends?—an observation
with a troubling consequence. If God has no friends, and if humans
are supposed to aspire to being godlike, then there is something fundamentally askew with Aristotle's whole picture.

Aristotle's Theological Questions

It is of course impossible for someone to be her own friend: by definition, friendship is the love of another human being on account

of that person's goodness. Nonetheless, Aristotle discerns analogies between self-love and friendship. Think of your soul as having parts. (Aristotle even has names for the parts: the vegetative soul includes such things as breathing and digestion; the appetitive soul includes such things as self-control, justice, and liberality; and the rational soul includes our intellective powers.) If the soul's parts fit together harmoniously (so that you do what you want to do, and you don't do what you don't want to do, contra Saint Paul's description of his own experience in Rom. 7:15), then your soul as a whole is living in something like friendship with itself. As a friend wills for his beloved the things that are good, not for his own sake but for the sake of the beloved, so in a good person, each part of the soul wants the good for the other parts and, most of all, wants the good for the whole person.

This is only an analogy, but it has its uses. It points to why wicked people are unable to be real friends with anyone. A bad person is someone whose soul lacks proper unity, which is to say, integrity; a bad person's inner constitution is unruly or disharmonious. People like that, lacking the good, cannot enter into (and certainly would lack the character strengths to persevere in) friendships in the proper sense.

But if a good person is someone whose soul is rightly ordered, is not such a person then self-sufficient? Why then would a good person need a friend?

It is because, as Aristotle sees it, humans live in groups but do so distinctively. He famously defines the human being as a political animal, one who dwells with others of its kind in governed societies ("cities"—*poleis*, from which we get "political"; see his *Politics* 1253a). As social beings who treat with others, a mark of a good character is justice, the acquired excellence of treating others rightly. Using an expansive understanding of friendship, Aristotle says, "All justice is about relations towards a friend." That is to say, with regard to every person with whom we have dealings, there can be something like friendship, a "civic friendship." Then he goes further and says that even family relationships are friendship. In sum, friendship is the special way that humans are social, or "gregarious."

> For justice concerns individuals who are partners, and a friend is a partner either in one's family or in one's way of life. For human beings

are not just political animals [i.e., living in governed communities], but also domestic animals [living in domiciles, i.e., households]; they are not like other animals who copulate in season with any chance female or male. No, humans are not solitary animals, but gregarious in a special way, forming partnerships with their natural kinsfolk. Accordingly, even if there were no such thing as the state, there would be partnership and justice of a sort. A household is a kind of friendship.

So we are political *and* domestic animals, "not solitary . . . but gregarious in a special way" (1242a20–28).

But a problem still lurks here. For regardless of the political arrangement (monarchy, aristocracy, republic, etc.), all civic friendship, both political and domestic, necessarily will be less than primary friendship. For civic friendship is a friendship based on utility; it comes from our need of others to accomplish living. Civic friendship is based on our lack of self-sufficiency.

Is then friendship a crutch, preventing us from developing true human greatness, keeping us from becoming as godlike as possible? Such questions force Aristotle to his final topic.

God, he says, "lacks nothing," and therefore "he will not need a friend," and furthermore, "since he does not need one, he will not have one." And from this, Aristotle admits the devastating human corollary: "Consequently, the happiest human being will have very little need of a friend, except to the extent that self-sufficiency is not possible." This means that a very good person will have very few friends, and the better the person, the fewer the friends. "He will not be eager to make friends, and will disdain not only friends for utility but also friends for company" (1244b8–14).

But that conclusion is unacceptable. It is contradicted by the obvious pleasure we have in our friends, a pleasure that is concomitant to their goodness quite apart from their usefulness to us. How did the argument reach such an erroneous conclusion? Where was our reasoning misled? Aristotle says it happened in "the comparison" (1244b23)—namely, of human beings to God. God, Aristotle holds, is not like us. God has no awareness of the world; he thinks only upon himself, and he is the first cause of all the movement in the world just by his being. Aristotle teaches that the universe is eternal and

uncreated—it was just always there. God causes all the movement in
it (this includes life and thought) not by doing anything, and certainly
not by any attention from himself toward the world, but rather by
the world's attraction to the transcendent beauty and goodness and
simplicity of God, the unmoved mover, who is, simply and entirely,
thought thinking itself.

So, yes, we are indeed attracted to God—that attraction is the root
cause of everything we do—yet we are attracted, Aristotle must say,
precisely as human beings. Human life is an activity that consists in
"perception and knowledge, and consequently sharing life is sharing
perception and sharing knowledge." We share life with one another;
God shares life with no one. God knows nothing but himself; he
never thinks of anything else (according to Aristotle). We obviously
think about many things and desire to know many things. But we
are like God to this extent: for us humans, "self-perception and self-
knowledge is the most desirable of all things"; indeed, for human beings, "living must be regarded as a kind of knowing" (1244b25–29).

Aristotle's argument here is a condensed form of his epistemology
(his theory of knowledge)—no easy subject! Yet it is not hard to get
a sense of it. If you are my friend, then you somehow enter into me,
and I into you. I will know you, and you will know me, and my own
self-perception and self-knowledge will include your perception and
knowledge of me, and vice versa. This is the highest form of what
happens in all human knowing, for knowing always involves taking what we know into ourselves in some way. In a revealing aside,
Aristotle observes that this is how "sexual love resembles friendship,
for the lover wants to share the life of the loved one, though not as
ideally he ought, but in a sensuous way" (1245a24–26).

He writes in beautiful words, "We all find it pleasanter to share
with our friends to the best of our ability the good things that fall
to the lot of each of us: in the one case bodily pleasure, in another
artistic contemplation, in a third philosophy. We need to be near
to our friends—there is a proverb 'friends afar a burden are'—so in
this shared activity we must stay close together." And a bit later he
says, "It is evident" that friends "should live together, and that this
is the dearest wish of everybody, and especially of the person who is
happiest and best." Thus, he concludes, the analogy with God breaks

down. The premise was "because God is not of such a nature as to
need friends, the same must be true of one who resembles God."
Yet this would also mean that "a virtuous man does not think of
anything," because God thinks only of himself, "being, as he is, too
grand to think of anything else." But manifestly, a virtuous man
does think of things that are outside himself, and he needs friends.
"The reason is that *for us well-being involves something other than
ourselves*, whereas he [God] is his own well-being" (1245a20–24,
b10–11, 15–19, emphasis added).

But note this. If, contrary to Aristotle's assumption, God were the
creator of the world, if God gave any of his attention to the world, if
God wanted to communicate with the world in any way—if any or
all of these were true, then we would not have to conclude that the
analogy with God is faulty. That is to say, if Aristotle's understanding
of God had been different than it was, then the way might have been
open to conclude *both* that Aristotle is right in his fundamental lin-
eation of friendship *and* that friendship is not just a human thing
but a divine thing.

Can God have friends? And can we be in their number? That
quest is the heart of this book. I want to know what friendship is
and to enjoy friendships in this primary sense: to be good, to have
good friends, and to have friendships grounded in the good. At the
same time, I would like to be friends with God. If these are things
we want (if indeed you want them with me), are they possible? How
might they be?

Theology and Friendship

Let's review where we are. At the end of his teaching about friendship,
Aristotle makes it clear that what we think about God can change
what we think about friendship. His prime mover (as he calls God)
is vastly different from the God of the Scriptures. The prime mover
has no relationship to the world. He is not the creator of the world;
the world has eternally just been there. Yet without doing anything,
the prime mover causes all the motion (all the life) in the world because all movement of any sort comes ultimately from the world's
desire for God.

Friendship, involving activity, is, like every activity, caused by this desire, and ultimately this desire is to be as much like God as we can be. Our desire for friendship is a form of our general desire for God; God has no friends; thus we desire, in friendship, a state of being that has no friendship. But such a conclusion runs against Aristotle's analysis of what it is to be an excellent human being. We are political and domestic animals, social beings who thrive in cities and households. Our pleasure—our excellence—is found, more than anywhere else, in our friendships.

Here resides an oddity in his thought. On the one hand, when he looks at human beings, Aristotle sees the formation of friendships as the epitome of human flourishing. On the other hand, when he looks to the prime mover, he sees there no place for friendship. Despite this, all the life in the world (all its movement) comes from the world's attraction to God.

For Christian theology (and in this there is no fundamental difference from Jewish theology), we will see there is no such oddity. But first—before we dig into that mind-blowing possibility, unimaginable to Aristotle, that God could have friends—let us consider more closely the difference between Aristotle's God and the creator God revealed in the Scriptures.

THREE

Friendship as Success at Being Human

The Strange Creator

Let's go back to the beginning—not our beginning but *the* beginning. It has been called a Jewish discovery that the world is created.[1] "In the beginning," the first book of the Bible begins, "God created . . ." Textually, it is not clear how to take that opening prepositional phrase. We might have an affirmation here that there was a beginning to things and that at that beginning God created. Alternatively, the text might be affirming not that there was a beginning but rather that at the root of all things (or the most essential thing to say about all things) is God, who created them.

We recall that Aristotle did not think the world was created and did think it was eternal both in past and future time. But once the notion of creation was in the air, philosophers started asking if the notion of infinite past time was a coherent, thinkable notion. Some, including notable medieval Islamic philosophers, thought the notion fundamentally incoherent.[2] There cannot be past time, they thought, because if there were, it would have taken infinite time to get to the present day. And that would mean there was an actual infinity in time. Actual infinites, however, are impossible, for the following reason. We can have potential infinites: we can, for instance, always imagine living for another day, and then another, and then another,

29

without end. Or (to take yours truly's nightmare version) we can always imagine having more cats. But we cannot imagine having actually lived an infinite number of days (or living with an actually infinite number of cats).[3] Similarly, we can imagine the US federal deficit increasing without bounds. It was a trillion dollars not that long ago, it is over fifteen trillion today, and possibly at some future time it will be more trillions than whatever number you would like to name. Nonetheless, the debt can never become actually infinite. No one, not even the government of the United States, can have an infinite debt. Actual infinities cannot exist.

So, the argument says, the world must have had a beginning. From this point, the argument goes on to say that it must have been created, and therefore God exists.

But Thomas Aquinas disagreed, interestingly so. He said that to have a beginning and to be created are different things. If we say the world is created, we need not also say it had a beginning. One might imagine this as a state of affairs in which, to put it roughly, "there was always a yesterday." More precisely, we could say that at any time in the universe's history, there could have been a predecessor time, that the universe always had a past. I think this is a philosophically coherent notion. It does not mean there has been actually an infinite number of past moments but only that no moment had no predecessor.

So there is philosophical disagreement. If we follow Aquinas' thinking, two conclusions follow immediately. The first is that we are free to turn over the question of the universe's beginning to whatever insights scientific inquiry might uncover. The current view, as I understand it, is that our universe did in fact have a beginning and it was about 13.8 billion years ago, and that our universe is expanding and will do so without end. But whether there was anything before that beginning some 13.8 billion years ago (the so-called big bang) is an unanswerable question. There might have been a previous universe that collapsed into the singularity that exploded in that big bang; if so, all information from it—every trace of its existence—would have been obliterated in the explosion that began our known universe. And furthermore, there might have been several, even uncountable, previous universes that expanded and recollapsed. Thus it seems that in principle, based upon contemporary scientific understanding, we cannot know whether the universe had a beginning. It might have, and it might have not.

But second, none of this undermines the doctrine of creation, for to create something means to give it existence. And to give existence is not necessarily to start but rather to hold in being exactly what exists for however long it exists. Which is to say, if it is a coherent notion to say "a universe without a beginning," then God could have created "a universe without a beginning." (The only reason God cannot create a square circle is that the words "a square circle" have no meaning—they are incoherent.)

The Jewish discovery of creation goes hand in hand with the discovery of the strangeness of God, for what is meant by "creation" is a radical distinction for which God is responsible: the distinction of creator and creation, a distinction that escapes all our attempts to specify it in language. This is why the Jewish religion forbids idol worship. Other religions of the ancient Near East worshiped the sun and the moon. Genesis 1:16, by contrast, insists that "the greater light" and "the lesser light" are creations of God (significantly, the text refrains from naming them). Sun and moon are demoted from quasi-divine status. They don't even appear until the fourth day. Sun and moon, land and water, cockroaches and cockatiels, human beings and the things their hands make and the words their mouths utter and the ideas their minds form are all creatures, creations. None of them is divine, none of them is creator, none of them is to be worshiped.

To create, properly speaking, is not to manufacture. The human being is a maker, *homo factor*. We make things out of other things. A chair, say, is made out of wood; a melody, out of pitch and rhythm. But wood, sound waves, the pulsations of time—these are already there before we step in to do our making. By contrast, to create is to give existence to wood and pitch and pulsations—and indeed also to the people who work with them—to give them existence for as long as they exist, exactly as they exist.

Another way to get at this is to recognize that the creator is not a countable thing in the world. You never look around a room and say it contains four chairs, five hundred books, three persons, and also, by the way, the creator. Incidentally, this is why the creator is singular. You could have five hundred books (indeed, you could have five tons of books), you might even have two cats (although I'd rather just stick with the books, thank you very much), but you could not have two creators. To be plural is to be countable, and there is no sense in counting God.

To see this yet another way, if we take the universe with its tons of books and myriad cats and everything else and hold it together in our minds as one very big thing, we cannot then imagine that God is "outside" it as another thing. We might speak of the "great divide" that separates creator from creature, yet it is actually not a divide in any thing. "Creator" and "everything that exists" cannot be united as two things put together: "It is not possible that God and the universe should add up to make two."[4]

But once we see the strangeness of God as creator, it is natural to think of him[5] as distant. Aristotle's prime mover, after all, is distant— and indifferent to the universe to boot. But the creator has no place, and therefore it does not make sense to say he is far away. Yes, God is not in the universe—he is not a thing among other things, a being among beings—yet neither is he outside the universe. He is strange!— the notions of "inside" and "outside" don't apply to him. But this means that, awesomely, he is "closer" to us than anything else could be. God is your creator who holds you in being, gives you existence, makes you *you*, for however long you have your being. He is closer to you than any other person could be, more intimate than your next heartbeat.

This strangeness of God the creator would seem to make the problem of friendship with God even worse than it was for Aristotle (for whom already it was impossible). How could God the creator be the friend of a human being? How could any of us have a friend who is nothing in the universe? How could my friend be the source of my existence? How could a created being have any relationship at all with the creator, not to mention a relationship of friendship that seems to involve mutuality and equality? There are hints in the Scriptures that these problems will not prove insuperable, and in due course we will have to see whether any sense can be made of the notion of being a friend of God. For now, we merely underline the point that, unlike Aristotle's prime mover, the creator is hardly ignorant of or indifferent to the world if the world is indeed a creation. God surely was not under any compulsion to create; yet once having made himself creator, he has tied himself to his creation as the continuing source of its being. Holding things in being, for as long as they have being, does seem to be some sort of relationship, even though it is unlike any other (for all other relationships are among creatures). This radical departure from Aristotle, this strange creator God, just might in the end be capable of friendship with human beings.

How to Make Friends (An Insight from Plato)

If God is the source of existence of all things (which is what we mean when we say he is the creator), then we can study those things on their own terms (without being immediately concerned about their relationship to God). In particular, we may understand human friendship as *something created*. God has given us a creation that has friendship in it; he holds the activities of friendship in existence just as he holds the friends themselves.

Ancient Greek wisdom has still more to teach us about friendship (even though it has no sense of God as creator). For a complementary view, I will turn from Aristotle to his teacher, Plato, who has a cunning illumination of how friendship is made. Plato was a master dialectician who wrote, for the most part and famously, *dialogues*, that is to say, conversations, searchings, pursuits. You can think of Plato's dialogues as being explicitly what other truth-seeking writings are implicitly; Plato puts the back-and-forth of thought into the writing itself. This is of great importance for us, for although it is seldom remarked, it is plainly there for us to see: in nearly every dialogue, friendship is Plato's implicit subject. The characters in the dialogues are (with some admitted exceptions) people who are trying to seek the truth—or should be! And to seek the truth in this manner presupposes a trust in the forthrightness and integrity of the others in the dialogue. That is to say, truth-seeking participants in a dialogue are people who could well be friends—people who, by that very process, might be already on the way to becoming friends.

The Platonic dialogue form displays human knowledge as a dynamic activity, a point that is made by Aristotle (e.g., that friendship is an activity as much as a state) but not illustrated and perhaps not sufficiently emphasized (and an essential point for those who would seek friendship). Here is the problem. Although human life is an activity, when we speak of Aristotle's ideal "virtuous person," we tend to omit activity from our mental picture of her, erroneously imagining someone who statically possesses human goodness. Thus when Plato constructs a written drama in thought in which people seek to know *what is the case* (about whatever they're talking about) and *how they should live*, he presses upon us vividly the essentially dynamic character of human beings and human thinking. Human goodness, Plato shows us, is not something we can lock up and put in the bank; we might have it in some partial way, yet it remains something we must also continue to seek.

Plato has one short, often-overlooked dialogue whose explicit subject is friendship. This is the *Lysis*. When I was an undergraduate at St. John's College, we spent many seminars on Plato's "Great Books," but the *Lysis* was not among them. It is reckoned a lesser dialogue; the classicist Edith Hamilton, for instance, opines that the *Lysis* is unsuccessful and that its importance lies not in its subject, friendship, but in its exemplification of the Socratic method. This conclusion misses the point. People may skip over the *Lysis* because it fails to achieve an understanding of friendship; indeed, at the end of the dialogue, having rejected every view he considered, Socrates admits defeat: "We have not as yet been able to discover what we mean by a friend" (223b).[6] But, as the philosopher Mark Vernon argues, to dismiss this dialogue in this manner is to overlook how it provides implicit teaching on what friends do and what they are about.[7] To state it sharply, when we examine Socrates' method, we are examining how friendship works. The Socratic method is a method of building friendship. Thus it would be no accident at all that a short, inconclusive dialogue on friendship would at the same time be an exemplary dialogue for the Socratic method, for that method is in fact about friendship.[8]

The *Lysis* opens with Socrates walking just outside the walls of Athens, where he falls in with some young men. The one who speaks to him, Hippothales, is in love with a juvenile, Lysis (we may think of Lysis as a young teenager, still under the care of a family governor).

Socrates owns that although there is almost nothing he has knowledge about, he has "received from heaven the gift" of discernment about love (204c). We learn elsewhere that a heavenly oracle spurred Socrates to seek wisdom; to be a philosopher is to be someone who loves wisdom, the paradox being that if you love wisdom, you have a longing for it, and if you have a longing for it, that means you lack it (one does not long for something one already has). Just so, later in the *Lysis*, Socrates makes the surprising claim that "the good" (meaning people who have wisdom) cannot be "friends to wisdom [philosophers]." The wise are not philosophers! Philosophers are people who, while not evil, still lack the good—that is to say, wisdom (218b).[9] Socrates, a friend of wisdom, knows about longing for wisdom—and therefore he knows about love. Behind all this, of course, is Plato showing us dynamism of human living and thinking.

The reader quickly sees that, by contrast to Socrates, Hippothales doesn't know the first thing about love, and moreover, damningly, he lacks any particular knowledge about the object of his desire, Lysis. He is merely infatuated, and he carries on in such an embarrassingly imprudent way that he is all but certain not to obtain his object. Socrates, who knows something about love, offers to demonstrate "a specimen of what you ought to say" (206c).

They enter the palaestra (wrestling school). Socrates takes note of Lysis' attractiveness, that he is "unmatched in face or form . . . not beautiful merely, but even of a noble mien" (207a). Lysis comes over to join Socrates, as do a number of others, including Lysis' cousin and friend, Menexenus. Socrates speaks first to Menexenus, asking if the two of them dispute about who is older or better or more beautiful. When they laugh, Socrates says he won't ask them who is wealthier, "for you are friends, are you not?" "Oh dear, yes!" they answer, and when Socrates notes that friends share their goods with each other, they agree (207c).

Shortly, Menexenus is summoned away, and Socrates turns his questioning to Lysis but along a new line. He brings Lysis to see that although his parents love him and thus want him to be happy, they constrain him as if he were a slave, not allowing him to do as he pleases. The questioning goes on for a few pages, leading finally to the awareness that it is when we have understanding (and are seen to have it) that people entrust things to us and we are "free ourselves in these matters" and also "lords over others," but with those matters about which we have no insight, we will not be allowed to do as we please and "will be subject to others." But if that is the case, asks Socrates, "Will anyone, then, count us his friends, will anyone love us in those matters in which we are of no use?" (210b–c). It is a devastating conclusion—Lysis agrees to it, but it means that his parents do not love him, and indeed it means that all love in the world is based on usefulness and that there is no difference between what is useful and what is good.

Here Socrates pauses in an aside to note something he didn't say. It would have been a "blunder" to say it aloud, yet still he wants us to know, us who are hearing his report of this dialogue: "This is the way . . . you should talk to your favorite, humbling and checking, instead of puffing him up and pampering him" (210e). One might read this as simple expedient advice: speak this way if you want to make a love conquest. But, alternatively, it might be that Socrates is saying, instead of trying to make a love conquest, try to turn "your favorite" into your friend. And the way you make a friend is through honest interest in the good of the person who is in front of you, and that honest interest will take you to "humbling and checking" instead of dishonestly flattering him. If the Socratic "method" is to make an interlocutor see that he doesn't know what he thought he knew, it is also to make him see that he has in you one who has his true good at heart—one who would be his friend.

When Menexenus returns, Socrates shares with him that from childhood he has preferred having friends to having good food or riches, even all the gold of the king. "On seeing, therefore, you and Lysis, I am lost in wonder, while I count you most happy, at your being able, at your years, to acquire this treasure with such readiness and ease—in that you, Menexenus, have gained so early and true a friend in Lysis, and he the same in you—while I, on the contrary, am so far from making the acquisition, that I do not even know how one man becomes the friend of another" (212a). This (slightly ironic) passage begins the latter half of the dialogue, in which Socrates ultimately gets them to realize that, though they think of themselves as friends, they no more know what friendship is than he does.

Finally, the dialogue ends, seemingly abruptly, as the governors of Menexenus and Lysis appear and take the boys away. Its inconclusiveness suggests that friendship is never wrapped up but is something human beings should continue seeking throughout their lives. I noted at the outset Socrates' avowal of their failure "to discover what we mean by a friend." He is saying they have failed as he is calling out to them as they leave. But his words imply something more complex than mere defeat: "Well, Lysis and Menexenus, we have made ourselves rather ridiculous today, I, an old man, and you children. For our hearers here will carry away the report that though we conceive ourselves to be friends with each other—you see I class myself with you . . ." And only at this point does Socrates assert they have not "been able to discover" the meaning of friendship. The dramatic truth must not be overlooked. In the very act of avowing a failure of discovery, *at that moment* the establishment of some ground for friendship is proclaimed. The three are embraced in a single action, one that outsiders may well judge "ridiculous": "we . . . I, an old man, and you children." Socrates puts himself together with them, across a vast age difference, and claims that they, all three, do think of themselves as "friends with each other" (223a). If they agree, then the course of the dialogue has somehow begun a friendship, and the end is a picture of beauty and hope that goes beyond the dialogue's sober words of having fallen short.

The Socratic method is a friendship method. It originates in a mutual desire for the truth, which corresponds to Aristotle's understanding of friendship in the primary sense as being about the good. Its parties must respect each other and not engage in flattery, even as Aristotle distinguishes real friendship from that which is about pleasure or utility. Friends are to make us better, and Socrates demonstrates that through the dynamism of dialectic. And while Aristotle said friends must be equals, Socrates shows that the equality in question is a willingness to seek the truth. Friendship does not demand equal experiences, or equal liberty (the boys are, after all, still under governors), or equal age.

When I read the *Lysis*, I wonder if what I need to do in order to develop friendships is to seek the truth boldly in honest conversation with others, even if they are vastly different from me in age or other matters. Indeed, in the process of writing this book, I often told people I was trying to understand friendship, and sometimes we just right then settled down to a long conversation about it. It is a wonder that precisely through such conversation one can start to become a friend, even while not knowing what friendship is! Friendship, it seems, truly is an activity; to be a friend is to do certain things. This valuable insight is our gift from Plato.

FOUR

Friendship and Beauty

Let Us Note Beauty

The action of the *Lysis* takes off from the beauty of Lysis the boy and the erotic or passionate desire for him, which Socrates then transforms. There is no life without encounter with beauty. Elaine Scarry, a scholar of aesthetics, spoke (forgive me if I say "beautifully") about this subject in her Tanner Lectures at Yale. Beauty apprehended moves us to replicate it—in words, in sketches, in sketches that we re-sketch or then write about. One sees a beautiful scene, one writes a poem, one then writes a commentary on the poem. This replication goes on without end. It encompasses even the simple act of staring, the desire to keep the beautiful object continually before oneself. Scarry tells us "that Leonardo, as though half-crazed, used to follow people around the streets of Florence once he got 'glimpses of it [beauty] in the strange eyes or hair of chance people.'"[1] And it extends to the desire of procreative union, that the beautiful one might be replicated in the flesh.

When Socrates first sees Lysis, he agrees that the youth has beauty to be remarked upon, but instead of showing Lysis' would-be lover, Hippothales, how to get Lysis into his embrace, he takes us all on a dialectical search for the truth about friendship. That search fails, yet the process itself prepares the participants for what might become

39

a friendship. Rather than Socrates becoming Lysis' lover, Socrates joins Lysis and Menexenus as a friend alongside them.

The question is, What sort of replication is this? If beauty causes us to desire to replicate it, the Socratic response seems to be that beauty is best (or at least better) replicated not in a sexual union but in a friendship that is achieved, if we may put it this way, asexually. This is another point on which we may find ourselves grateful to Plato. The dialogue shows no queasiness around sexual liberties and yet seems to suggest a human fulfillment that is sexually abstinent. That is to say, there is no anxiety here about sexual relations (and not just same-sex relations but man-boy relations), and yet there is a definite preferencing of friendship that is not paired (there are three of them) and is not sexually consummated. Is the best way to replicate beauty found in friendship? Is Socrates suggesting that beauty can spur us to our highest activity when it spurs us to make friends? Would he wish to train our eyes so that we see beauty most of all in friendship?

How Many Friends Can Someone Have?

Dialogues—conversations—take time. We pause to consider further Aristotle's point that we can't have a large number of friends because it takes time to test out and form friendships. In 2018, a professor at the University of Kansas published the results of his research, said to be the first of its kind, into how much time forming a friendship actually takes. The study measured hours spent together ("hanging out" and the like) and found that "it takes roughly 50 hours of time together to move from mere acquaintance to casual friend, 90 hours to go from that stage to simple 'friend' status and more than 200 hours before you can consider someone your close friend."[2] These results, of course, could be challenged for sampling bias (perhaps too many students) and the subjectivity of the difference between the various levels. In addition, common sense would say there can be no hard-and-fast correlation between the closeness of a friend and the quantity of hours spent together. Nonetheless, we do have here a reality check. Two hundred hours is roughly seven hours every day for a month. That large quantity of time is said to be needed just to *establish* a close friendship. To go further and *maintain* the friendship would take additional, ongoing time. It is ridiculous to think one can have very many friends. I remember as a young boy overhearing my farmer-grandfather tell his son-in-law (my father) that a man has only six people he can count on if he gets in serious trouble. The mind of a young boy wondered, *Only six?* But the mind of a widower might wonder, *As many as six?* Yet it is also ridiculous to think of forming friendship as merely spending time hanging out together. The key question concerns what is done during that time. Is the friendship based on the good? Are the friends themselves people who desire to be good and to know truth? Yes, time matters, and it is sobering to realize how much time is required. But activity also matters, and the content of that activity. Which is to say, theologians and philosophers can learn from sociology, but sociology will not give us the last word.

Cicero: Friendship's Rare Beauty

One last time we turn to a classical thinker, a Roman who famously held friendship to be rare and exalted. He is the statesman and philosopher Marcus Tullius Cicero. Shortly before his death in 43 BC, Cicero wrote *Laelius de Amicitia*, a work that claims to be Cicero's memory of Scaevola (an old man whose student Cicero had been about forty-five years earlier) recounting a conversation that he, Scaevola, had had with Gaius Laelius in the year we know as 129 BC, "just a few days after the mysterious death of Scipio Minor." The *De Amicitia* is thus a doubly remembered conversation. The friendship of Scipio and Laelius was widely acknowledged and held in high esteem; consequently, when the opportunity arose shortly after Scipio's death, it was natural enough for Laelius to be pressed by two sons-in-law to speak to them about what friendship really is. In the main, the *De Amicitia* contains this remembered discourse on friendship by Laelius. I will consider the teaching that Laelius sets forth to be Cicero's account of friendship; indeed, it has commonly been taken as such by subsequent writers (one of whom, the twelfth-century Aelred of Rievaulx, plays an important role later in this book). Cicero's teaching, we will see, has commonalities with that of Plato and

Aristotle, yet in "arrangement, plan, style and illustrations," he is
doing something new—something of beauty, done, as W. A. Falconer
wrote nearly a century ago, with unmatched "charm."[3]

Since it is through his mastering rhetoric that Cicero teaches, there
are rewards for taking the dialogue slowly, savoring his elevation of
the truths of friendship.

The "whole essence of friendship," he says early on, is "the most
complete agreement in policy, in pursuits, and in opinions" (iv.15),
which is to say, "an accord in all things, human and divine, conjoined
with mutual goodwill and affection [*benevolentia et caritate*]" (vi.20).
Laelius, having known such extensive agreement and harmony with
Scipio, expresses the hope that the memory of their friendship will
endure always; it matters more to him even than that his reputation
for wisdom would last. Is this because there have been more famous
wise men than famous friends? He says at least this much: "In the
whole range of history only three or four pairs of friends are men-
tioned; and I venture to hope that among such instances the friendship
of Scipio and Laelius will be known to posterity" (iv.15).

Friendship is rare and exalted. Only those who are good can become friends. What is its root? It arises from a certain fact about
human nature, those ties we have to one another that are strengthened
by proximity. Nature brings us to give preference to our fellow citizens, neighbors, and relatives. But what arises from those proximate
ties generally does not amount to friendship; such ties can survive
without goodwill, whereas for friendship, goodwill is of the essence.
Thus friendship excels all other relationships. Although there are
"infinite ties uniting the human race," ties that are "fashioned by
Nature herself," friendship is something much narrower, more re-
fined: "The bonds of affection always unite two persons only, or, at
most, a few" (v.20).

Rare, exalted, grounded in nature, limited to no more than a few
people, friendship gives us the occasion to "repose on the mutual
goodwill of a friend," without which life would not be worth living.
There is nothing "sweeter than to have someone with whom you
may dare discuss anything as if you were communing with yourself,"
someone to share your joys and also help lift the burdens of adversity. In this, friendship, although rare, reaches wide. It "embraces

innumerable ends; turn where you will it is ever at your side; no barrier shuts it out; it is never untimely and never in the way" (vi.22). It "excels all other things" by projecting "the bright ray of hope into the future," not suffering "the spirit to grow faint or to fall." To look "upon a true friend" is, in a way, to look upon an image of yourself. "Wherefore friends, though absent, are at hand; though in need, yet abound; though weak, are strong; and—harder saying still—though dead, are yet alive" (this spoken by one whose dear friend died just days before; vii.23).

And friendship is widely acclaimed. In a new play written by a "guest and friend" of Laelius (it becomes a story told through the ages, thanks to Cicero), it came about that one Orestes was to be put to death, but the king could not execute the sentence because he did not know which of two friends was Orestes. When he commanded that Orestes step forward, both arose at once, each saying, "I am Orestes!" Orestes' friend, Pylades, did not want Orestes to die; Orestes did not want his friend to die in his place. Each thus showed himself willing to die in his friend's stead. At this moment in the play, Laelius reports, "The people in the audience rose to their feet and cheered." Although the audience, he laments, would lack the courage to imitate this self-sacrifice in their own lives, nonetheless nature in them "asserted her own power" as they approved what they saw performed in drama as human greatness precisely in friendship (vii.24).

Friendship is built into our human nature, but where? It does not arise from our mere neediness, the human weakness and want that drive us to seek proximity and community. Neediness, weakness, and want, Laelius has already noted, can exist without goodwill, but there is no friendship without goodwill. Etymology unpacks the connection: *amicitia* (friendship) comes from *amor* (love). It is a love that establishes goodwill, "an inclination of the soul joined with a feeling of love," an inclination that arises from meeting "someone whose habits and character" attract us not because (or not only because) we find such habits and character "congenial with our own" but because in this person we "behold, as it were, a sort of lamp of uprightness and virtue." Virtue is attractive: nothing, according to Cicero's teaching, "more allures us to affection" than virtue (viii.27–28).

So it would be wrong to claim that friendship arises out of mere need, for the wise, as is commonly said, need nothing, yet nonetheless they treasure their friendships. Laelius cites a friendship he had with Africanus. Neither of them had any need that the other supplied. "I loved him because of a certain admiration for his virtue, and he, in turn, loved me, because, it may be, of the fairly good opinion which he had of my character; and close association added to our mutual affection" (ix.30). Even—perhaps especially—virtuous and wise persons enjoy mutual love, share a common admiration for that which is virtuous, and enjoy close association with one another. Of course, advantages then follow, but it is not for the sake of those advantages that friendship comes to be.

Most people find it hard to have friendships that endure to death. Here is Ciceronian realism grounded in the tumultuous public and political life of Rome. Countless contingencies intervene; parties may cease to be advantageous to each other, or their politics may diverge; the burdens of age may make a past friendship impossible to maintain. And, if we may import the word, sin can get in the way, for it might turn out that one's friend asks one to do something wrong. Laelius is clear that friendship can never excuse wrongdoing; above all, it cannot justify a wrong against the commonwealth. So there is a law in friendship: "Neither ask dishonourable things, nor do them, if asked" (xii.40). But to rest here would be to focus overly on the prohibition; Laelius restates the law positively in order to show that what friends should do for each other goes far beyond the avoidance of things dishonorable: "Ask of friends only what is honourable; do for friends only what is honourable and without even waiting to be asked; let zeal be ever present, but hesitation absent; dare to give true advice with all frankness; in friendship let the influence of friends who are wise counsellors be paramount, and let that influence be employed in advising, not only with frankness, but, if the occasion demands, even with sternness, and let the advice be followed when given" (xiii.44).

To foreclose the possibility of having to endure the breakup of a friendship, either under the contingencies of life or the exposure of a friend's lack of virtue, one might think it better to try to live without friends. This, however, is humanly devastating; to thus "deprive life of friendship" would be "to take the sun out of the universe." It is also, as a general point, self-contradictory to avoid occasions wherein one's virtue could be put to the test; virtue is obtained and grows in us precisely when we meet trouble and then, through "rejecting and loathing" the things that are contrary to virtue, thereby grow in kindness, temperance, bravery, justice, and so forth (xiii.47). Furthermore, virtue is not hard in every part of life; "especially in friendship," virtue "is so pliable and elastic that it expands, so to speak, with a friend's prosperity and contracts with his adversity" (xiii.48).

To have friendship that endures is to have friendship that is knit together by virtue. Therefore friends must exhibit some shining virtue from which love springs forth. Good people will love and join themselves to other good people. This is far removed from mere expediency, which would remove "from friendship's chain its loveliest link." For we do not delight in the gain that we may obtain from a friend but rather in "his love, and his love alone" (xiv.51). Advantage attends on friendship, not vice versa.

Everything hangs on the friends having, and seeking to have, good character. When their characters "are blameless, then there should be between them complete harmony of opinions and inclinations in everything without any exception."[4] And when character falls short, Laelius finds room for accommodation. Should a friend wish for something that is "not altogether honourable," if he nevertheless is desiring of and seeking to have good character, it may be that we should for his sake (his life or reputation, say, being at stake) "turn aside from the straight path," provided that it will not lead to "utter disgrace" (xvii.61).[5]

Laelius finds it astonishing that most people know exactly how many goats or sheep they have but cannot say how many friends they have—that they take "pains to get the former" but are "careless in choosing the latter" (xvii.62). How then should one go about securing friends? They need to be tested; we should not be like fickle children who quickly take on friends without considering their character. One looks for loyalty in a friend, because loyalty is a sign of a friend's potential for constancy over time. One also looks for a friend to eschew feigning and hypocrisy and to avoid suspecting that the friend has done wrong; such behaviors of openness manifest goodness and wisdom. One looks too for a certain affability of speech and manner.

Should one seek out new friends? Not necessarily, for old friends are not to be despised. Yet new friends are not to be scorned if they offer hope of becoming good friends. There must be equality among friends, and so if one is superior to the other, he should treat the inferior as a superior in order to manifest their equality. (Laelius gives examples of Scipio doing this in xix.69.) And, perhaps obviously, decisions about friendships require that one be oneself a person who has matured with strength and stability of body and mind. The problem that Cicero seems to have in view is that "ungoverned goodwill"—which could go back to one's childhood, when one had not yet developed virtue—could get in the way of one doing what one should do with and for one's friends. One needs also to be able to endure "the temporary separation of friends" when separation is a matter of duty; dishonorably refusing to part would be another instance, it seems, of "ungoverned goodwill" (xx.75). Thus friendship's ongoing exercise requires virtue, even as its coming into being was through attraction to the friend's virtue.

Sometimes one must break off a friendship, but if so, it should be done gradually, if possible. The sole security against the ills and annoyances of friendships that must be broken off is "neither to enlist your love too quickly nor to fix it on unworthy men" (xxi.78). It is, it seems, necessary to give thought to the various ways friendship can fall short. But it is unsatisfactory to conclude with thoughts of failure. So Cicero turns the end of his work back to an exhortation to attend to virtue, which is necessary for our happiness and indeed without which we cannot obtain friendship. Friendship is essential to human life, for if someone had every desired material thing in the world, if she were completely alone, deprived of all human intercourse, her condition would be most unendurable of all. Since, therefore, "things human are frail and fleeting, we must be ever on the search for some persons whom we shall love and who will love us in return; for if goodwill and affection are taken away, every joy is taken from life." In a supremely eloquent affirmation of the classical ideal of friendship, beyond the distinction of private and public, of

action and rest, of engagement and study, grounded in virtue and
ever seeking virtue, Laelius gives us our final words:

> Of all blessings that fortune or nature has bestowed on me, there is none
> which I can compare with Scipio's friendship. In it I found agreement
> on public questions; in it, counsel in private business, and in it, too, a
> leisure of unalloyed delight. . . . There was one home for us both; we
> had the same fare and shared it in common, and we were together not
> only in our military campaigns, but also in our foreign tours and on
> our vacations in the country. Why need I speak of our constant devo-
> tion to investigation and to learning in which, remote from the gaze
> of men, we spent all our leisure time? . . . I exhort you . . . so to esteem
> virtue (without which friendship cannot exist), that, excepting virtue,
> you will think nothing more excellent than friendship. (xxvii.103–4)

FIVE

The Weirdness of Divine Love

Fundamental Theology: Jesus "Reveals Man to Man"

We turn now to some basic claims made in Christian theology. Section 22 of *Gaudium et spes* ("Joy and Hope," one of the most important decrees of the Second Vatican Council of the Roman Catholic Church, 1962–65), begins with a bold one: "The truth is that only in the mystery of the incarnate Word does the mystery of man take on light. For Adam, the first man, was a figure of Him who was to come, namely, Christ the Lord. Christ, the final Adam, by the revelation of the mystery of the Father and His love, *fully reveals man to man himself* and makes his supreme calling clear."[1] The mystery of what it is to be human—the mystery that we meet whenever we meet a human being—is fully seen only in the mystery of the incarnate Word, that is to say, in Jesus of Nazareth. *Gaudium et spes* here explicates the thought of Saint Paul (a footnote directs us to Rom.

When I speak of God's love for us as "weird," I mean that it is not only mysterious, unusual, or strange but also in a sense "uncanny," beyond our "ken." God's love does not fall into any category (just as God himself cannot fall into any category): it is weird, and while the most wonderful thing in the world, it is also unsettling. Job must have felt this weirdness when the voice spoke to him from the whirlwind! On the other hand, I repudiate any sense of the "weird" that involves fate or the loss of freedom (as in the "weird sisters" of Shakespeare's *Hamlet*). God's love liberates us—another aspect of its surprising strangeness, as we will see.

5:14, although the argument extends from verse 12 through verse 21). If we translate the Latin *homo* as "human" taken as a noun, we could say that the first human, Adam, is a figure of the final (*novissimus,* newest or latest, ultimate) Adam. And that final Adam, Jesus Christ, fully manifests the human to the human.[2]

Dear reader, here is a sad truth: you and I fall short of being humans. We own up to this when we admit to being sinners. Sin is not something we add to ourselves and need to get rid of (although it can feel like that; our sins constitute a "burden" that "is intolerable," according to a traditional prayer, and the Epistle to the Hebrews speaks of "the sin that clings so closely" [12:1 NRSV]).[3] Rather, sin actually is a defect, a falling short on our part of living up to our nature, a failure to be human in the full sense. We sinners, who live among sinners, never have seen in the flesh a totally real human being. The astonishing claim is that Jesus is the one, true, complete human being.

So when we say that Jesus is like us in all things except sin, we are not saying that we have something, "sin," which Jesus fails to have. It's the opposite: Jesus has something that we do not have—namely, full humanity from which nothing has been broken off and taken away.

And yet, sinners that we be, we do have Jesus. *Gaudium et spes* 22 makes another remarkable claim: "By His incarnation the Son of God has united Himself in some fashion with every man."[4] This teaching was frequently cited by Pope John Paul II in his anthropological/ christological re-presentation of Catholic social teaching. John Paul emphasized that the dignity of every human being comes from a union with Christ—a union that is there even when that person is unaware of it and even prior to any missiological announcement of the gospel.[5] How it is possible for this to be true is a project that theologians continue to work on. Yet in whatever way the theology works out, these two claims will remain foundational: (1) only in Jesus can we see what true humanity is, and yet at the same time (2) Jesus has "in some fashion" (*quodammodo*) united himself, already, with every human being.

This means that "in some fashion" what we are looking for, when we seek to understand friendship (or anything else about being humans), is already there, because even though we are sinners and thus less than fully human, in every instance the human being has been united with Jesus, the Word of God in the flesh, who is the one fully human being. Nevertheless, what we seek can be seen in truth only in the light that is shed by that same Jesus.

What Christianity gives us is the interpretive principle: to see what a real human being is, we must look to Jesus. I said earlier that the doctrine of creation—the discovery that God is the creator giving existence to everything that is—can give us confidence to study friendship without particular reference to Scripture or some other divine message. To this we may now add that the doctrine of the incarnation can give us confidence that when we study human things, there is a certain graced reality already there (because the incarnation means that Jesus has already united himself, somehow, with every human being). But the recognition that we are sinners must significantly caution our study. For when we look at friendship in the world—in philosophical thought, in our own experience, and wherever else—we are not looking at full humans. We need the light of Christ in order to see our true humanity.

To put this in one sentence, we will need to look to Jesus if we are to understand what friendship is in the fullest sense.

God's Love

Friendship is a kind of love, so let us think for a bit about love.

It's considered unproblematic and almost trite to say that God loves people. But actually "God loves people" is nearly the strangest of all possible sentences. This idea is not something the Bible gets to quickly or easily. One does not find the word *love* at all in the creation stories that open the book of Genesis, or in the stories of the flood and the tower of Babel, or in the stories of Abraham, until God tells Abraham to sacrifice his son Isaac.[6] Here is the first appearance of "love": God identifies Isaac as "thine only son Isaac, whom thou lovest" (Gen. 22:2). This first instance of love is parental; it may be that it is noted in order to emphasize the radicalness of the filial sacrifice.

Isaac, perhaps because he was almost sacrificed by one who loved him, seems to have more of a need for love than any person before him. When he takes Rebekah to be his wife, we are told "he loved her" (Gen. 24:67), and not much later we are told he loved his elder son: "Isaac loved Esau . . . but Rebekah loved Jacob" (25:28). And unlike anyone else up to this point, Isaac is also said to have a love for something (as opposed to someone): he is known for his love for "savoury meat" (27:4, 9, 14)—a love that plays in a famous deception scene.

Late to appear, love continues in Genesis as something problematic. Jacob's love for Rachel but not for Leah causes intrafamilial discord. Shechem's love for Dinah threatens Israel's integrity and leads to violence. Israel's (Jacob's) love for Joseph over his other sons precipitates their jealousy—and so forth. As a whole, the book of Genesis seems hesitant to speak of love, knows love only as something between humans (except for Isaac's love of savory meat), and presents it as a source of strife or a sign of blindness. *Nowhere in Genesis is love connected with God.*

The first claim that love might be connected with God is in Exodus, when God gives the Decalogue, specifically in the commandment not to make graven images. God says he is jealous but also merciful, "shewing mercy unto thousands of them that love me, and keep my commandments" (Exod. 20:6). These words presume that it is possible to love God, and they suggest that those who love God and keep his commandments could constitute a large number—namely, "thousands." But once stated, this claim of the possibility of human love for God does not reappear in the canonical order of Scripture for a long time. Interhuman love, however, is spoken of in increasingly positive terms. For instance, a servant might attest to his love of "my master, my wife, and my children" (21:5). For interhuman love, the supreme command, of course, is to "love thy neighbour as thyself" (Lev. 19:18; cf. 19:34).

Only when we get to Deuteronomy do we find it said, finally, that God can and has loved people. Moses tells the Israelites that God chose them "because he loved thy fathers" (Deut. 4:37; note that Israel is being taken as a singular, "thy"). Looking back as it were to Abraham with his wife, Sarah, and their descendants (but not, it seems, to the descendants of Abraham through Hagar or Keturah), Moses interprets God's call of them, and all that God did with them, as his love for them: "He loved thy fathers." This leads naturally to a repetition of the claim of his mercy toward those who love him (5:10, reprising the comment in Exod. 20:6 noted above) and to the command to "love the LORD thy God with all thine heart, and with all thy soul, and with all thy might" (Deut. 6:5). Whereas in Exodus it is not said that God loves people (although he does show mercy to "thousands" who love him "and keep [his] commandments" [20:6]), in Deuteronomy it is said plainly. God loves the people he has chosen (chap. 4), he shows mercy to those who love him in return (chap. 5), and the love of God, the keeping of his commandments, is to "love the LORD thy God with all thine heart, and with all thy soul, and with all thy might" (chap. 6).

Why do the canonical Scriptures unfold with this initial reticence to speak of love, particularly of the love of people for God and, with even greater reticence, the love of God for people? It is clear that the Bible invites us to ask this question, for the question lies implicit there in the text. But it is also clear that the Bible does not give an explicit answer.

There is, however, a clue to be found in the context. We note that it is in the midst of the promulgation of the Decalogue that we are first told that God will show mercy to those who love him (and thus that it is possible for people to love God). That is to say, it is precisely when God is giving the law to his people that he speaks of people loving him.

What might we make of this? Although it was necessary for God to promulgate the law for his people, that necessity had a tragic character to it. In fact, all law has a tragic character. We must have laws against identity theft, for instance, only because people steal identities. It would be better if there were no stealing! But once a law has been promulgated, people will be tempted to think that simple obedience to the law is enough. However, it is not enough for us merely to avoid stealing from one another!

Divine law partakes of this tragic character. One cannot relate to God merely as a matter of external obedience. It is not sufficient, for instance, to avoid making idols; one needs to relate positively to God, and that is to love him. The true keeping of the law is accompanied by love.

But I think something even deeper may be going on here. Perhaps the emergence of love is brought about not only as the necessary counteraction to external legal obedience to the law that God has spoken but also as something that God makes possible by his speaking anything at all—that is to say, only in a context where God speaks to people is it possible for people to love God. The Scriptures seem to demonstrate that God must first speak to us before we can love him. Obviously, he spoke to Abraham. And then half a millennium later, God spoke to Moses, and at that time, in the context of giving the commandment to love him, revealed that he had loved Abraham. But why would we need God to speak to us before we could love him?

The Creator Cannot Love His Creation

You cannot love something that is fundamentally unequal to you. If something is immensely more powerful than you, your love is going to be that of a timid servant to an overbearing master. Such servants always know that at any time the master could crush them.

If something is immensely weaker than you, your love will always be mere benevolence, a bestowal of "charity" that cannot help but perpetuate, to some extent, the existing inequality between you and the object of your benevolence.

If I say I love my cigar, and you ask me why I love my cigar, and I answer that it's because it has such interesting things to say, you will likely ring up my bishop and tell him he has a problem on his hands.

Nietzsche famously rejected God because no matter how well-intentioned God might be, the divine-human relationship would always be a master-slave relationship. If God is the creator of the world, God is fundamentally unequal with his creation, and therefore he cannot love it. Love demands that the parties somehow be on an equal plane.

To shift the analogy, think of the relationship of an author to the story she writes. The author could be very pleased with her story. She could find herself thinking all the time about her characters and the lives they lead. But if she claims, say, to be having a picnic with one of her characters, it's time for us to call the proverbial doctors. And if she writes a story in which the characters claim to be talking to her, we would probably find that really weird. A few authors have ventured such stories. In *The Comforters*, for instance, the magnificent Scottish novelist Muriel Spark has one of her characters hear an unseen typewriter clicking. That character comes to realize that she has an author and that she is incapable of escaping from the novel she is in. She hears a sort of chorus (the author's?) say exactly what she herself is doing. The character never gets to talk with her author—she can't. And she quite resents being trapped in a story.

Here's the point: to claim that God loves people and that people can love God is to make the claim that, in some sense, God and people can be equal, on some sort of equal footing.

The Bible's implicit claim then, which gradually dawns upon us as we read it in its canonical order but which is finally clear in Deuteronomy, is that *God is more than our creator*. He doesn't only hold us in existence. He also somehow makes it possible for us to love him, and that is because he has loved us all along.

If God speaks to Abraham—if indeed God and Abraham can have a conversation—then somehow God and Abraham are on the same level. That means that God has lifted Abraham up from the level of being a creature only or that God has become more than merely a creator.

That God and Abraham speak with each other is a significant point of the narrative from Genesis 11:27 to 25:10. It takes a while, but finally God reveals his mind to Abraham, stopping by his tent, receiving his hospitality, and at last asking (the question is posed so that the reader will understand), "Shall I hide from Abraham that thing which I do; Seeing that Abraham shall surely become a great and mighty nation, and all the nations of the earth shall be blessed in him?" (18:17–18). On one level, God is saying that he will educate Abraham in the ways of being a ruler, which is important because through his people all the people of the earth will be blessed; therefore, his people must be governed well. Abraham needs to learn hard lessons about judgment and how the law always, unavoidably, brings bad consequences. (We need, for another instance, laws against murder, but sometimes the guilty will go free and more innocents will be harmed by them, and sometimes the innocent will be caught up in the punishment of the guilty. It is impossible to mete out justice perfectly.)

But there's more, I think. All the nations of the earth are going to be blessed through Abraham because God, talking with Abraham, puts himself and Abraham on the same level. Abraham, that is to say, is a blessing because he shows everyone who has ears to hear that conversation between God and a human being is possible. So from these early chapters of Genesis the Scriptures make it clear that God is an author who wants to be a character in the story he has created. And that, of course, is what he finally brings about in the fullest sense in Jesus.

But God the Creator Does Love, and Speak

Implicit in the (very strange) claim that God has spoken to people is the possibility of people being given by God the ability to be on some sort of level with him. This same implicit possibility lies behind any claim that God loves people. God's speaking and God's loving thus come to the same point: verbal intercourse between the creator and the creature.

This is beyond our understanding. We cannot see how an author could become a character in his story, nor how a character could come to speak with and love and be loved by her author. There are interesting efforts in fiction and film to explore this possibility—in film, I recommend *Stranger Than Fiction*—but they always fall short of showing its consummation.

Still, there are many things in Christian faith that are beyond our comprehension, and yet we hold them to be true. The greatest of them all is the claim that Jesus Christ was dead on Friday and alive on Sunday.

We would have to reject the claim that God speaks with and loves people if the claim were a contradiction: contradictions are incoherent things (like square circles) and they cannot exist. And it would be a contradiction to say that Muriel Spark really communicated with Caroline Rose, the principal character of her novel *The Comforters*. In fact, if a character in a novel had, in the novel, a conversation with her author, the "author" in the novel could not be the same as the actual author of the book. Any real conversation between character and author would always slip away and be unachievable, because it would be a contradiction.

Yet it is not a contradiction to claim this about God because God is not a created thing. Muriel Spark is a creature, and her novels are themselves creatures. And a creature that is a human being cannot be identical with an idea (another creature of a sort) that is put into a novel any more than, to repeat an example I have used in an earlier book, Fred could be at the same time both a man and a duck. (He could be half-man and half-duck, but he couldn't be fully man and fully duck. Humans and ducks are both creatures; to be two different kinds of creatures at the same time and in fullness is impossible.) But Jesus can be God and human at the same time because to be God is not to be a creature. So it cannot be proven to be a contradiction for *God* to be both creator and creature. Nor need it be a contradiction for *God* to be both author and character.

However, if we did not have the revelation to which the Scriptures attest, we would have no reason to say that God has spoken to his people, has loved and desired to be with his creation, and has finally become one with us. There is no necessity to any of this, it is a weird thing to say, and we do say it only because (we believe) it has happened.

What then has happened with regard to friendship? The next chapter will follow the unfolding of friendship, through the Scriptures, both among humans and between humans and God.

SIX

Biblical Friendships

Friendship with God

Two individuals in the Bible are celebrated as being friends, or holding a place as a friend, of God. With Abraham, the language is unequivocal: he was a friend of God. The attribution of friendship is retrospective; in Genesis itself, where the story of Abraham unfolds, we do not find the claim of friendship. But later, in the strengthening words from God to his people that open the second part of Isaiah, we find this assurance: "Thou, Israel, art my servant, Jacob whom I have chosen, the seed of Abraham my friend" (41:8). So does God comfort and upbuild his people by identifying them as the descendants (in a collective singular "thou") of his friend, Abraham. In a reciprocal discourse, in the writings of the chronicler, the people make their plea to God in these significant words: "Art not thou our God, who didst drive out the inhabitants of this land before thy people Israel, and gavest it to the seed of Abraham thy friend for ever?" (2 Chron. 20:7). In this plea for God to act, the people make bold to identify their ancestor Abraham as God's friend.

There is equality in friendship, as we saw Aristotle insist and as we have claimed is involved in love in general. Friendship also opens the way for a claim to be made upon the friend. Because God had a friendship with Abraham, his "seed" can advert boldly to that friendship for God's continuing action on their behalf. And conversely, God, seeing the people in need of comfort, reminds them that they are descendants of his friend.

That Abraham was God's friend in this unique way—namely, that he alone in the Scriptures is spoken of as "the friend" of God—continues even to the late writings of the New Testament. In the Epistle of Saint James we find, "The scripture was fulfilled which saith, Abraham believed God, and it was imputed unto him for righteousness: and he was called the Friend of God" (2:23). Here it seems to be almost a title for Abraham and at the same time a summation of his life. The first scriptural appearance of love was when God told Abraham to sacrifice "thine only son Isaac, whom thou lovest" (Gen. 22:2); the ensuing action was the climax of Abraham's life of listening to God and being the father of a new people. The listening and being are summarized by James as "believing," which gets counted as "righteousness." All this is wrapped up in the single word *friend*. Friendship with God is the ultimate characteristic of the father of God's people.

Moses, whom we might call the second founder of the people Israel, is likened unto a friend of God, although he is not said explicitly to be such. This simile, however, is not made retrospectively but comes rather as a contemporary description of Moses' conversations with God. "And the LORD spake unto Moses face to face, as a man speaketh unto his friend" (Exod. 33:11). This is said only once—in keeping with the general reluctance of the Old Testament to use friendship language between humans and God. But at the same time, it is decisive in holding up the high standard: if someone is going to be God's friend, that person must have open discourse with God. Anything less would not be worthy to be called friendship.

Human Friends: David and Jonathan?

It is often said that the Bible's great model of human friendship is the love of Jonathan and David. But a close reading makes that claim questionable. The actual word *friend* is not there.[1] More importantly, the love that is shown in the text is unbalanced: it is mostly Jonathan's love for David, with the Scriptures being significantly silent concerning whether and how David responds. As we will see, it is clear that Jonathan loves David, but the converse is at least an open question. Biblical narrative tends toward reticence, generally telling us only what people say and do. It is silent about their thoughts and motivations, yet those can be signaled by what the text does not say.[2] We first see Jonathan in a battle. It is the second year of the reign of Israel's first king, Saul, who is Jonathan's father. Jonathan with a thousand men "smote the garrison of the Philistines that was in Geba," and at Saul's command a trumpet was blown "throughout all the land," and "all Israel heard say that Saul had smitten a garrison of the Philistines" (1 Sam. 13:3–4). The text says that Jonathan did the smiting, while the report from Saul's command is that Saul did it—foreshadowing a strain between father and son that will mark all that follows and revealing as well Saul's unfitness for the kingship.

Shortly thereafter, when the Philistines have gathered against Israel in frightful numbers, Jonathan ventures a courageous move. Going alone and secretly, he says to his armor bearer that "there is no restraint to the LORD to save by many or by few" (1 Sam. 14:6). In the event, the Lord saves by few: Jonathan and his armor bearer alone slay about twenty men, and their unexpected and successful attack sends a "trembling" throughout the Philistines, who begin to run away. Saul's army sees the enemies' flight, runs after them, and wins a victory. But Saul puts an oath of fasting upon his army, which Jonathan unwittingly breaks and thus brings upon himself a curse: a second incident of the father working against his son and a further sign that the king is unsuited to his position. When it is revealed that Jonathan is the one who has broken the oath (an oath he knew nothing about and, when learning of it, declared unwise), Saul pronounces, "Thou shalt surely die, Jonathan" (14:44). But the people argue a bit of sense into Saul and rescue Jonathan, thus saving the hero of the day from death.

David enters after the narrative has decisively established the unfitness of Saul. His entrance is twofold.[3] First, he enters Saul's court as a man "who is a cunning player on an harp" and who thereby can dispel Saul's evil spirits. Saul "loved him greatly; and he became his armourbearer" (1 Sam. 16:16, 21). But he also enters in the story of Goliath (chap. 17), courageously risking an independent action much like Jonathan's. These two stories together establish David as someone with a spirit like Jonathan's but who, unlike Jonathan, can master Saul's passions and receive Saul's love. The text emphasizes David's cunningness through all this. Before he takes up against Goliath, he repeatedly asks, and repeatedly hears, the things Saul has promised to the man who defeats Goliath: "The king will enrich him with great riches, and will give him his daughter, and make his father's house free in Israel" (17:25; cf. vv. 26, 30). His repeated questioning, when he already knows the answer, shows David to be not only the beautiful musician but also someone alert to seize his chance.

This cunning, in a word, is the problem with seeing the relationship of Jonathan and David as a biblical model of friendship. Even when David is publicly emotive and the hearts of many go out to him, we cannot forget his shrewdness; and while Jonathan clearly loves David, it is hard to find in the text clear evidence that David returns this love. The strongest protestation of love for Jonathan is in the poem that David composed to mark the death of Saul and Jonathan, a poem that is state poetry for public consumption (2 Sam. 1:19–27).[4] It shows David as magnanimous to his enemies: it is a performance that he cannot but know will lift him in the eyes and affection of his people. "The beauty of Israel is slain upon thy high places: how are the mighty fallen!" (v. 19). The poem nobly links together Saul and Jonathan with prowess in fighting, with courage; they were "lovely and pleasant in their lives, and in their death they were not divided" (v. 23); they were like eagles and lions. This is manifestly less than the whole truth, as we know all too much of Saul's failures, and we remember his conflict with his son established in the text from the beginning. The poem speaks of Jonathan alone only toward its end: "I am distressed for thee, my brother Jonathan: very pleasant hast thou been unto me: thy love to me was wonderful, passing the love of women" (v. 26). Yet even this affectionate, presumably heartfelt, and public language of "brother" and "love" contains ambiguities, for the entire David narrative makes it clear that David's love of women is often instrumental.[5] Moreover, when David speaks of the love of women *for him*, we note that even here David's speech is of Jonathan's love *for him*. We find, at best, a slight attestation of David's love for Jonathan: "Very pleasant hast thou been unto me," a love for him that was "wonderful." And that's all.[6]

It would be wrong to exaggerate all this into a one-sided portrayal of David as a heartless, feeling-less, Machiavellian calculator. A good deal of what people loved about David was that they saw him openly passionate, for instance, when dancing in front of the ark (2 Sam. 6). But we must also note the places where the Scriptures are silent about David's love. At the beginning of 1 Samuel 18, we find, "The soul of Jonathan was knit with the soul of David, and Jonathan loved him as his own soul." It is not said that David loved Jonathan. Two verses later, it says that Jonathan and David made a covenant, "because he loved him as his own soul." Again, although a covenant is a mutual agreement, the text does not say that David loved Jonathan. Jonathan gives David his robe and his sword and his bow—princely gifts—but no reciprocal gift is made: the imbalance makes it look like Jonathan is giving his kingly inheritance to David (and indeed he says explicitly later, "Thou shalt be king over Israel" [1 Sam. 23:17]). In chapter 19 we read that Jonathan "delighted much in David" and thus would not kill him, as Saul ordered, but we do not read that David delighted in Jonathan. In chapter 20, we read, "Jonathan made a covenant with the house of David" that David, when God had defeated all his enemies, would show "the kindness of the LORD" to him and would kill neither him nor his descendants (vv. 14–16). And Jonathan made David swear that he would not kill him, because Jonathan loved him "as he loved his own soul" (v. 17). Again, this stands without a counterbalance, as nothing is said of David's love of Jonathan. Jonathan is helping David survive the deadly anger of Saul; David obviously needs that help, but he does not express love. Only at their parting is there reciprocity: "David arose . . . and they kissed one another, and wept one with another, until David exceeded" (v. 41). Yet even here, what immediately follows are words of Jonathan's, his reminder of the vow they made according to which David would not kill Jonathan. In their final meeting, when Saul is at war seeking David's life, Jonathan comes to David to strengthen "his hand in God," and they make a covenant before the Lord (23:16–18). This, at last, is truly reciprocal and political; it is Jonathan's reminder to David of their previous promise, which is now strengthened, even as Jonathan is undermining his father's battle.

To work through all these details is to see how difficult it is to claim (no matter how often one hears the claim repeated) that the Bible

portrays David and Jonathan as exemplary friends. It seems plausible
not only that David was truly "distressed" at his loss of Jonathan
but also that Jonathan had been useful and pleasant—important
elements of friendship but not, on David's side, the highest.

Yet if we look elsewhere, we can indeed find a strange and important depiction of friendship in the Bible, one that is often ignored.
It involves Job.

Job: The Bible's Picture of Real Friendship

The book of Job is wildly misunderstood and hugely underestimated
for its human wisdom—that is to say, its godly wisdom about what
it means to be human. At least in significant part, it is a book about
real human friendship (and a hint of divine). If we read it with the
question of friendship in mind, it will show us that friendship is difficult, that friends should be tenacious, and that friendship is the
best thing in human life.

Friendship's importance is flagged from the outset of the book.
Catastrophic things happen to Job. "Job's three friends heard of all
this evil that was come upon him," and immediately they went to
him "to mourn with him and to comfort him" (Job 2:11). When evil
strikes, the appropriate thing is for friends to gather round. And the
task of friends is, first, simply to be with their friend in trouble, "to
mourn with him"; but their task is also to build up or strengthen
their friend, "to comfort him" (remembering that "comfort" means
to strengthen; it draws from *fortis*, Latin for "strong" or "brave").

In the event, Job's friends are able to do only the first. They mourn
with him. They are in fact so affected by the sight of him in his trouble
that they are speechless: "They sat with him upon the ground seven
days and seven nights, and none spake a word unto him" (Job 2:13).
The friends do not presume to try to comfort him with words that,
assuredly, would be inadequate to the evil that has befallen Job. I
marvel at their silence, their waiting, their mournful solidarity—this
is a good model of true friendship.

It is Job who breaks the silence. The disputes for which the book is
famous occur only after their joint silence and Job's cursing of the day
of his birth. The responses of Job's friends, the offense that they take

to his words, his counter-responses, their escalating disagreements—all this is too complex for us to work through in detail. It is enough to note that they do not run away from but stick with each other, albeit increasingly convinced that the other is wrong on some of the most serious matters of life. Even at the end of speech—"So these three men ceased to answer Job, because he was righteous in his own eyes" (Job 32:1)—his friends do not leave him. Silent they may be to the end of the book—and mistaken! But they do not leave their friend Job.

At the climax of the book, "the LORD answer[s] Job" (Job 38:1), which is what Job has wanted all along—to speak with God as a man speaks to a man, not, does he say, as a friend to a friend but as a person in court can put questions and demand answers. But the answer the Lord gives Job is not an answer to his questions, explicit or implicit; it is something altogether unexpected. "Gird up now thy loins like a man," God says (38:3)—Robert Sacks of St. John's College points to a Hebrew particle here that suggests an invitation, as if God were saying "please."[7] God, inviting Job to rise up to his humanity, addresses questions to Job—"Where wast thou when I laid the foundations of the earth?" and so forth (38:4)—but Job of course cannot answer. The effect of the questions is to elevate Job out of his human-centric world and take him on a tour of the universe, from its beginning to the present. It is as if Job is carried back to the big bang and asked what his role in that had been, as if God takes him through the vast expanses of the empty space of the universe to the galaxies and dust and strange things that humans never see, as if God shows him how the universe at large is no place for a man to be.

At the end of Job's journey he beholds Leviathan. This wild beast is untamable. He cannot be spoken to. He will not play with Job. He is utterly indifferent to the world and literally impenetrable. God shows him to Job and asks, "Canst thou fill his skin with barbed irons?" (Job 41:7). The question is rhetorical; Leviathan has a hide that is impervious to harm. And Job surely reflects on how different he is from this Leviathan: he, Job, a human being, has a skin that can be eaten away with disease and sores—can be, and has been. Job is not impervious. He is a human being, and he is vulnerable.

What Job sees, in other words, is that while there is no explanation to be given for the evils that come upon human beings (or at least no complete explanation of all the evils), there is still something wonderful about God giving people a place in the universe to live, a place where friendship is possible. And so Job returns to his home and does what is needed for that to happen. He recognizes (better than "repents"[8]) that he is—that all people are—"dust and ashes," and so he prays for his friends, the Lord accepts his prayer, and their friendship is restored.

The final scene of the book of Job is a picture of human communion. "There came unto him all his brethren, and all his sisters,[9] and all they that had been of his acquaintance before, and did eat bread with him in his house." Friends, family, and acquaintances, all together, all eating bread in Job's house. And what are they doing together? "They bemoaned him, and comforted him over all the evil that the LORD had brought upon him: every man also gave him a piece of money, and every one an earring of gold" (Job 42:11). What they do is what friends do for a friend upon whom evil has come—the intention of Job's friends in chapter 2 is fulfilled here in chapter 42. They mourn with him and they comfort him, they strengthen him in the very practical, material help of money and gold. But the comfort lies also in the recognition, and the acceptance, that the Lord did indeed bring evil upon him. The friends too have learned something. They do not deny that life is hard, that justice is not always obtained, that bad things happen in ways that cannot be explained. Unlike in their earlier speeches, here they accept hardship, evil, Job's innocence—they accept it all, and they are together with him in friendship, sharing company and food and, one imagines, stories and happiness.

I think Job's friends are able to accept the world as it is because Job has accepted it, has found a strange wonder in it. Job's reconciliation comes through what God showed him: that a human being is a little thing in the world, a precious thing with whom God is willing to talk, yet an exceedingly vulnerable thing, and thus what we need more than anything else is each other, is friendship. The book of Job ends with the news that Job gives an inheritance to his daughters along with his sons—the only instance in the Old Testament that daughters are treated equally with their brothers.[10] This is no accident: it flows from what Job has come to understand about the importance of human beings one to another. It is a concrete sign of the sort of change that can be brought about by the difficult achievement of friendship.

I believe the book of Job does not show us an answer to the problem of evil but rather an answer to the question of human nature. What are we humans really? Job says: we are precious beings, capable of discourse with God, beings who should strive to accomplish friendship with each other.

Friendship: The Mission of Jesus

In this way, Job is a preparation for the gospel, for the point of the incarnation is achieved when Jesus establishes friendship.

Friendship, one might think, seems a minor part of Jesus' message. We remember that Jesus was called "a friend of publicans and sinners" (Matt. 11:19; Luke 7:34)—a slur against Jesus that is reported ironically, for indeed he was a friend of sinners and people, like tax collectors (the "publicans"), who were despised. And there are instances of Jesus speaking positively of friends in some parables, for instance, the person invited to a wedding banquet who takes the lowest seat but then hears joyfully the words "Friend, go up higher" (Luke 14:10). Nonetheless, there seems to be much teaching about the kingdom of God that does not refer to friends, and Jesus' own ministry of calling the Twelve is generally taken to be the formation of a renewed people of God, or a school of disciples, students whom he is shaping to carry on his mission after he is gone—people over whom he is the head, not people with whom he is equal as would be a friend.

But if we go deeper, it becomes clear that establishing friendship was Jesus' mission. Saint John reveals friendship's centrality to what Jesus was doing in his account of the Last Supper, which takes up nearly a fourth of his Gospel (chaps. 13–17). Famously, John replaces the novel words of Jesus over the bread and wine with his equally novel washing of the disciples' feet. He establishes the context as one of Jesus' complete command of the situation. He "knew that his hour was come that he should depart out of this world." He had "loved his own which were in the world," and he is loving them "unto the end." The supper was ended, and Jesus grasped the entirety of his mission, "that the Father had given all things into his hands," that "he was come from God" and was going "to God." In this context, John shifts into the present tense, "He riseth from supper," as if to put us there on the scene. He "laid aside his garments" and then (present tense again) "poureth water into a bason, and began to wash the disciples' feet." When this was done, he took "his garments" and sat "down again" (13:1–12).

Saint John frames the footwashing event in the context of Jesus' self-consciousness of the incarnation as a whole: his coming from God and his return to God or, as we say, his being incarnate of the virgin Mary, dying, being buried, and rising again to ascend to his Father's right hand. He knows he has come from God and is going to God. The action in itself, however, is an interpretive mime of his immanent death and resurrection, as Saint John understands them. For this evangelist, Jesus' death does not come over Jesus, but rather Jesus lays down his own life. Jesus is in charge. After accomplishing his death, he takes up his life again. All this was laid out when he spoke of himself as the good shepherd (John 10:14–18). Just so, at the Last Supper, he lays aside his garments, which stand for his life, and when he has accomplished his purpose (here symbolized by washing feet), he takes up his garments again, as indeed he will rise on the third day.[11]

Following this action, Jesus speaks to his disciples. It is his last chance to shape them. He prepares them for persecution; he predicts his betrayal and Judas goes out, but no one save Jesus (and perhaps the beloved disciple) knows why; he strengthens their hearts and tries to lead their minds into the truth. At the end, he prays for them at length.

In the middle of these five chapters, at the center between the footwashing and the prayer, Saint John puts the central point of what Jesus has done with his disciples: "Greater love hath no man than this, that a man lay down his life for his friends." What it means to be a friend is to be willing to die for one's friends. Jesus is about to die, and he makes it explicit for his disciples: "Ye are my friends." He then goes on to make a point about this friendship that is consonant with the classical saying that friends share all things: "Henceforth I call you not servants; for the servant knoweth not what his lord doeth: but I have called you friends; for all things that I have heard of my Father I have made known unto you" (15:13–15). That is to say, the friends of Jesus share Jesus' mind. Everything his Father has told him—all of that is now known by Jesus' friends. Indeed, that is why they are friends.

When Jesus tells the disciples they are his friends, he adds what looks like a conditional clause: "Ye are my friends, *if ye do whatsoever I command you*" (John 15:14). This is worth some thought. By what follows immediately (Jesus' explanation that they are not servants but friends because he has shared his mind with them), it is clear that whatever Jesus commands is something they will understand. Jesus will not command his friends as a servant might be commanded, where one might be told to do something without knowing why or what it is about. Jesus' commands are all intelligible.

This, by the way, is why hearing is at the heart of obedience. The "-edi-" in "obedience" is from *audire*, from which we also get "audio": obedience is about hearing with someone else (in hippie jargon, being tuned in to the same wavelength). I can recall my Oklahoma grandmother asking, "Do you hear me?"—meaning, did I understand what she wanted me to do. True obedience is not so much a bending of the will as it is a work of the intellect leading the will.

Furthermore, it is love and nothing else that Jesus has commanded: "This is my commandment, That ye love one another, as I have loved you" (John 15:12). So to live as friends, to demonstrate that greatest love, which is the willingness to die for one's friends, is what Jesus commands his disciples. But it is a commandment only in the sense that it points out what must be the case if we are Jesus' friends. The friends of Jesus are friends of one another and so are willing to die for one another. One cannot be Jesus' friend alone: "Ye are my friends," he says (v. 14); "ye are," plural, not "thou art," singular.

Following the revelation of friendship, Jesus returns to the love of one another, repeating it as his command and pointing out that, as his friends, they will share such hatred as he himself has borne. But as he has overcome "the world" (here to be understood as that part of creation in ultimate rebellion against God), so shall they. We find a similar point made by Jesus in Saint Luke's Gospel, in the one other place where Jesus calls his disciples friends: "And I say unto you my friends, Be not afraid of them that kill the body, and after that have no more that they can do" (12:4). The encouragement to face death, if necessary, is appropriately made to "my friends" by one whose executioners then had "no more that they [could] do."

Saint John shows us two additional and important elements of friendship with Jesus: it is personal, and it is expansive. I noted above that John's Last Supper account, covering five chapters, begins with the footwashing as a mime of Jesus' death and resurrection. This interpretation draws on the good shepherd discourse of chapter 10: "I am the good shepherd: the good shepherd giveth his life for the sheep. . . . I lay down my life for the sheep. . . . No man taketh it from me, but I lay it down of myself. I have power to lay it down, and I have power to take it again" (vv. 11, 15, 18). In that same discourse, Jesus emphasizes his personal relationship with the sheep, the sign of which is that he knows them by name and they hear his voice and follow him: "The sheep hear [the shepherd's] voice: and he calleth his own sheep by name, . . . and the sheep follow him: for they know his voice. . . . I am the good shepherd, and know my sheep, and am known of mine" (vv. 3–4, 14).

Significantly, the one instance Saint John gives us of Jesus calling someone by name, who from his voice and the spoken name recognizes him, does not involve one of the disciples—not even the beloved disciple, who had visited the tomb just before—but a woman, Mary Magdalene. She is distraught not only over Jesus' death but even more so over the loss of his body: "They have taken away my LORD, and I know not where they have laid him" (20:13). Jesus is suddenly behind her and asks why she is weeping, whom she is seeking. She takes him for the gardener and says, "Sir, if thou have borne him hence, tell me where thou hast laid him, and I will take him away." The narrative continues, "Jesus saith unto her, Mary. She turned herself, and saith unto him, Rabboni; which is to say, Master" (vv. 15–16). With these few words, Saint John brilliantly weaves together threads from the Last Supper and the good shepherd discourse: John 15 points to John 10, which then is fulfilled in John 20. Jesus, who lays down his life for his friends, has the power to take it up again and knows his sheep by name; they recognize him and are his. Here we see that Mary Magdalene is also one of Jesus' friends.

The friendship of Jesus is personal and expansive. There are always "other sheep" who also "shall hear my voice" (John 10:16). But although there are more and more sheep, there is never the distance of anonymity. Friendship is the intimacy of a common mind. Every one is known by name; every one who hears can follow; every one who follows is a friend.

To say it again: it is to establish friendship that Jesus undertook the incarnation, obedient to and fully comprehending of his Father's intention. He is of one mind with his Father, and his friends are of one mind with him, loving one another.

But Do We Want to Be Jesus' Friends?

The Gospel was from John 15, including the words "I have called you friends"; the occasion was the installation of the new dean of St. Matthew's, the Episcopal cathedral in Dallas. The preacher allowed that it sounds pretty good to be Jesus' friend. There are lots of perks: you get to be close to Jesus; you get to know what he is thinking. But then it might dawn on you that, as his friend, he can call on you anytime. You're never "off duty," as it were. If something is bothering Jesus, he is going to want to share it with you. If he is concerned about a family, worried about a child, thinking of someone who is alone, he might ask something of you. If he wants people to understand him better, to have a chance to move from ignorance into truth, he might call on you. You're his friend, right? To share the mind of Christ is to share so much: the burden of illness, of mental suffering, of confusion, of oppression. It is so heavy. It is a cross. It is a willingness to hand over one's life for the sake of the friend.

Do you really want that? Do we want it? Do I want a friendship that's sealed in death?

The Weird Intimacy of God

I think it is clear: the biblical revelation tells us that God sent Jesus in order to establish friendship with himself and among human beings. Yet while clear, it is not trumpeted; in fact, one must read the text carefully and trace certain threads across both testaments in order to grasp it. More traditionally, other scriptural themes and images are emphasized. The Bible is read as a narrative of creation, fall, and redemption. Redemption involves God's commitment to rescue and restore humanity from its self-wrought alienation from himself. In the catechism of the Episcopal Church, for instance, sin is said to have brought about disharmony, a fracturing of right relationships all around. As a result of sin, we humans are out of harmony with God, with one another, with the created world, and indeed even within ourselves. Salvation is the healing of these broken relationships, bringing reconciliation and peace with God, with one another, within our own persons, and with the creation at large.

"God was in Christ, reconciling the world unto himself," writes Saint Paul to the Corinthians. And the mission of reconciliation continues: God "hath committed unto us the word of reconciliation" (2 Cor. 5:19). Does speaking of friendship add anything to reconciliation?

It adds a dimension of depth, if friendship is understood in its primary sense. Friendship in all the forms it takes is primarily a love between people based on the good. So with regard to the created order and to our own internal order as persons, friendship would not be used in its primary sense. We can be in harmony with the creation, and we can have an integral personality without a divided will, but we can be friends properly neither with the ecosphere nor with ourselves. (The reader may recall, from chapter 2 above, Aristotle raising the question of self-love.) Yet when we turn to our relationships with other people, if the point of the incarnation is to enable us to live together as friends, that shows us the astonishing stretch of the gospel. Not just to live with others in a certain peace, not just to help others as best we can, not just to share the good and pursue it with those who are close to us but to have that closeness of common life and common mind with every other redeemed person (and not forgetting that we may dare hope that every person be a redeemed person)[12]—this is the specificity that "friendship" brings to the mandate of reconciliation. To love one another as Jesus has loved us, to see the explosive possibilities of "one another" being expanded without limit, and nonetheless not to water down this intimacy but to have it as friendship—all this is, it seems to me, weird.

Weird, and prima facie impossible. But before we draw back from this conclusion and dilute the gospel vision (making it something more palatable or "reasonable"), we must also note that friendship adds content to reconciliation—not merely clarifying it but saying more—when we are talking about reconciliation with God. It might have been possible for God to overcome our fall and restore us to a sinless state without making us his friends. God might have put us back in paradise without establishing friendship with us. It is conceivable to take the fall as our rejection of our place as creatures of God and our prideful attempt to usurp God's place as creator and then, in some way, to conceive our redemption as our restoration to our proper creaturely place. But this is not the story the biblical narrative tells. Rather, the Bible is a story of God wanting to love us, to speak to us, to raise us in some way above the level of creature so that we could speak to him and love him. Abraham his friend, and Moses, and the chosen people, and the prophets—all are there to show us this desire of God. Herbert McCabe claims that the most important thing Jesus says is that the Father loves him.[13] In Jesus, the love of God with a human being is consummated, made factual and actual, made real. Jesus as a real person in history established that it is possible for God and a human being to love each other. As Aristotle says, if it's actual, it's possible.

Weird as it may be, it is still true: we can be friends with God.

This double weirdness—of human friendship with God and of human friendship extended expansively to other people—is the point of the Bible. Yet it remains much less than perfectly clear. How, for instance, can we take friendship as the point of the gospel if Christian love is supposed to be love of everyone?

SEVEN

Christian Friendship and Christian Love

The Problem of Christian Love and Friendship

If friendship is the point of human life, we seem to have a problem with Jesus' rightly famous teaching that we should love our neighbor, indeed, that we should love even our enemy. It certainly seems that friendship and this commanded love (shall we call it "Christian love"?) stand at odds. Friendship is particular, but Christian love is universal. Friendship is reciprocal, but Christian love is unidirectional. Friendship is drawn to the good and thus discriminates, unlike the rain that falls on the just and the unjust alike. Jesus seems to teach against valuing friendship highly when he says, for instance, "Love your enemies, bless them that curse you, do good to them that hate you, and pray for them which despitefully use you, and persecute you; That ye may be the children of your Father which is in heaven: for he maketh his sun to rise on the evil and on the good, and sendeth rain on the just and on the unjust" (Matt. 5:44–45). The word translated "love" here is *agape*, and *agape* is generally taken as self-giving performed selflessly. It is taken as altruism, a turning to the other without regard to who the other is. It is said to act without regard for any internal attraction to the beloved, in distinction from erotic love, *eros*, which builds upon such attraction. And it is said to lack the particularity that characterizes *philia*, which is friendship. So how can we reconcile friendship, the reestablishment of which we have argued is the point of Jesus' entire mission, to this radical teaching on selfless love that Jesus says will make those who practice it the children of their heavenly Father?

Augustine's Theology of Friendship[1]

It is not a new question.[2] Aurelius Augustine (354–430), one of the West's towering theologians, made love a central theme of theology; in Augustine's hands, love explains God, history, and human beings. Love is the key for understanding the Trinity: the Father loves the Son, the Son receives and returns this love to the Father, and the Holy Ghost simply is that love. Furthermore, the contrast between two loves is the interpretive key to all human history: on the one hand, there is the city of God, which is grounded in love of God to the contempt of self; and on the other hand, the city of man, grounded in love of self to the contempt of God. Most personally, Augustine put love for God at the center of his theological anthropology. Each human person is fashioned to love God, a love that animates everything we do and that can be satisfied only by God himself.

Perhaps the most-read book ever, apart from the Bible, is the *Confessions* of Saint Augustine, which he wrote in the year AD 397 and in which he confesses love for God as he gives an account of his life up through his conversion and baptism (at Easter in AD 387, in his thirty-third year). The opening words of the *Confessions* give praise to God and are immediately accompanied by wonderment whether any human being can rightly praise God—for how can we know God without praising him? Yet how can we praise him rightly without knowing him? The first paragraph ends with the famous words that serve as the motif of Augustine's life (and that of many others who will find him, in the *Confessions*, as a type of themselves): "Our heart is restless till it rest in thee" (*inquietum est cor nostrum, donec requiescat in te*).

So do we see that love is central to Augustine's theology. But equally was friendship central to his personality. Throughout those decades in which he wandered before his heart could rest in God, Augustine had several close friendships, and he never outgrew his desire to cultivate and enjoy friendship. After he became a Christian, he insisted on living in community with friends, and as a bishop in northern Africa, he drew other clergy around him to live a rather novel form of common life at the cathedral. He had some close friends "from youth to old age," others who became friends later, with many of these friendships nurtured through his extraordinarily voluminous correspondence.[3] Augustine valued and cultivated friendships all his life.

The patristics scholar Joseph Lienhard identifies Augustine as the first theologian to work out a theology of friendship. It appears in the *Confessions* and perdures to the end of his life. True friendship is not a relationship based on sympathy or some other common ground. Rather, it is a divine gift; it is one way we experience God's grace. Friends are such because God's Holy Spirit has made them so, giving them the particular bond of friendship. "True friendship . . . is not possible unless you [God] bond together those who cleave to one another by the love which 'is poured out into our hearts by the Holy Spirit who is given to us'" (IV.iv.7).[4]

On the basis of this view, Augustine judges his pre-Christian friendships in stringent and even severe terms, because those friendships lacked this divine foundation. In book IV of the *Confessions*, we read about one particular, very close, very dear friendship that he had in his late adolescence. As was not unusual at the time, neither Augustine nor his friend had been baptized, nor were they desirous of being so, for they also shared a disapproval of orthodox Christianity. Then his friend took ill, and it was thought he might die. While he was in a fever and largely unconscious, his parents had him baptized (which also was not uncommon). After the friend recovered, Augustine visited him and launched into a mockery of the baptism as a meaningless ceremony. But his friend cut short such talk and rebuked him strongly. Augustine held his tongue, thinking that he would later find his friend in a more pliant mood—and then suddenly his friend died.

Devastation and grief overcame Augustine. His account of the experience must be reckoned to include some of the most beautifully poignant sentences ever penned about human loss.

> Everything on which I set my gaze was death. My home town became
> a torture to me; my father's house a strange world of unhappiness; all

that I had shared with him [my friend] was without him transformed into a cruel torment. My eyes looked for him everywhere, and he was not there. I hated everything because they did not have him, nor could they now tell me "look, he is on the way," as used to be the case when he was alive and absent from me. I had become to myself a vast problem. (IV.iv.9)

Augustine clearly wants us to learn something about friends and about God. Writing his *Confessions* as a bishop, he continues this remembrance through several additional, anguished paragraphs in which he describes and tries to understand the grief he felt at the time. At the end, he identifies the problem: he had loved his friend as if his friend would never die. But, he now says, that kind of love should be given only to God. He should have loved God first—although, being misinformed and foolish, he knew nothing about God. But if we love God first of all, we will be loving someone who never will die. And then we can love our friends "in God." This is Augustine's basic view of friendship and what he wants us to learn. We need first to love God and then to love our friends in God, who in fact gives our friends to us.

With these theological moves, Augustine secures a place for human friendship within Christianity. Where Aristotle or Cicero would place true friendship in the good of the friends and the good they desire, Augustine names that good as God himself and places true friendship "in God" and sees it, moreover, as a gift of God's grace. And to the question of how friendship fits with Christian love, if friendship is a bond that God has established, we need not worry that it will contradict the selfless and universal love that God seems to have commanded in Christ.

Yet one might wonder about the character of this friendship. Augustine secures friendship within an overarching love he has for God—a unidirectional conception, not the reciprocity we think of as characterizing friendship. Indeed, to love a friend "in God" seems to bespeak its own unidirectionality, a love toward the friend, a love that promotes the good of the friend, and so forth, without being a reciprocal love that also receives from the friend.

However, as Carolinne White points out, Christ's second love commandment (to love one's neighbor as oneself) works against

Augustine's Neoplatonist tendency to direct all love to God alone. If the neighbor must be loved, then Augustine's theology must have a place for love of people who are not God. The result is that one's friend cannot be eclipsed in one's love for God; one wants friends—neighbors, indeed any other human beings, even, as Augustine will remind us, one's enemies—themselves to love God. In other words, one wants other people to be "as oneself": people who love God supremely over all.[5]

Still, there is some weight to the charge of unidirectionality: How can we understand God's love for us, indeed God's friendship with us? Yes, he gives us grace, he gives us friends—but how is God himself a friend? For a theological understanding of friendship that pushes these thoughts even further, we turn to the second towering Western theologian.

Aquinas: Christian Love Is Friendship with God

Thomas Aquinas (c. 1224–74) makes a brilliant move when he declares that Christian love (*caritas*, the Latin equivalent of *agape*) simply is friendship (*amicitia*, the Latin equivalent of *philia*) with God.[6] It is a breathtaking thought that somehow the universal love that we might call "Christian love" or "charity" is nothing else but friendship with God. That is to say, despite all the differences between friendship and Christian love, between *philia* and *agape*, at their highest they are just one thing.

If Aquinas makes this claim, we can expect that he will work through the difficulties we have seen. And indeed he does just that.[7] To see how Christian love is the same thing as friendship with God, I will lay out Aquinas' thinking on friendship in terms of the principal suspicions or objections to which it responds.

To the objection that Christian love is extended to all people but friendship involves mutuality, Aquinas says that when we love a friend, we love everything about that friend. Thus our love will want to expand to include the friends of our friend, even if those friends have no other connection to us. "When a man has friendship for a certain person, for his sake he loves all belonging to him, be they children, servants, or connected with him in any way. Indeed, so much do we love our friends, that for their sake we love all who belong to them, even if they hurt or hate us."[8] So when we love God, we also love those whom God loves. Each human being is, potentially, a friend of God. So whenever one human being, a friend of God, is loving God, that love is naturally extended to all the other friends of God—that is, to all other people insofar as they are also friends or potential friends of God. This is why we love our enemies: they too belong to God in that God's love extends to his enemies also.

Then there is the objection that friendship, since it necessarily involves sharing because friends do things together and share each other's lives, cannot be the same thing as love of God, since human beings cannot have anything like a common life with God. This objection is based on the radical difference between God as creator and human beings as creatures. To this, Aquinas answers that charity/ love is God's gift, something that comes to us by grace, and once it has been given, then there is indeed some sort of transformation so that human beings can have communion with—share with, communicate with, have a sort of common life with—God. To repeat that Aristotelian adage, "If it's actual, it's possible." Weird and beyond our understanding as it is, Aquinas' point is that God has actually given the grace that makes it possible for us to have mutuality with him in love, a mutuality that is properly called friendship. "Charity signifies not only the love of God but also a certain friendship with Him . . . a certain mutual return of love, together with mutual communion. . . . Now this fellowship of man with God, which consists in a certain familiar intercourse with Him, is begun here, in this life, by grace, but will be perfected in the future life, by glory" (ST I-II.65.5).

The previous objection also needs to be faced with regard to friendship with other people. If friendship involves sharing one another's life, then it cannot be extended to a large number of people, since we are finite beings and cannot have a huge number of friends. But this seems to contradict Christian love, which is to be extended to all people. Aquinas answers that Christians truly will want to communicate with all God's friends, but they are not required to do specific acts toward every person, because it is impossible to do so (ST II-II.25.8). Aquinas expands this point into concrete advice. There is a sort of friendship with oneself whereby one seeks preservation particularly of one's spiritual goodness but also, in its proper place, of one's body. There is also a proper preference given to love of one's family. And there is a proper preference given to one's fellow citizens. One also should love (and will want to love) those who are close to God, those who are more fully realized as God's friends. How one sorts out these differing loves in concrete situations cannot be specified in advance; it requires that one practice and become skilled at making good practical decisions. The signally important point is to be disposed and ready to love *all* those whom God loves, to want to be friends with God and with *all* God's friends.

In similar fashion, it could be objected that friendship is truly friendship only when it is based on the good. One cannot be a friend with those who are not good in themselves and who lack a desire for the good. Yet Christian love is supposed to be directed to all people and particularly is not to exclude sinners and one's enemies. Aquinas answers that God has offered his friendship to sinners and to his enemies. Jesus was a friend of sinners (Matt. 11:19), and he asked that his own death not be held against those who accomplished it (Luke 23:34). The theological move here is to distinguish an offer from its actual reception. The offer of grace in Christ is universal; it is held out to all people (e.g., John 3:16). The reception of the offer of grace remains in the realm of human freedom, although, again, we cannot in the end understand how such an offer could actually be rejected— just as we cannot understand any particular sin.

As is often the case, here Aquinas is practical. It may not be required of us to show particular actions of love toward our enemies. For instance, they may be recalcitrant, or they might pose a threat to others, such that it would be harmful to them and others for us to do particular loving actions. Or it might be that in our weakness in this fallen world, we are unable to perform them. Nonetheless, Aquinas says, we do need to be ready to love them and to offer them friendship, in his words, "if the necessity were to occur" (presumably, if they were sincerely to repent!). Despite all this, Aquinas will not have us forget that in the perfection of Christian love, one does love one's enemies in appropriate particular actions, done apart from any necessity (ST II–II.25.8).

So friendship with God is, first, the grace given when God loves a human being. This grace makes possible a love for and with God. This is rightly called friendship, since love involves mutuality, communication, and benevolence. Friendship with God necessarily extends from God to all God's friends, which is to say, potentially, to all people. It also reveals a transformation of the notion of friendship in that, for a Christian person, friendship's longing is now universal, like God's. It extends not only to the virtuous but also to the wicked, not insofar as they are wicked, of course, but insofar as they are loved by God.

But how can friendship extend, even potentially, to all people without lessening its intimacy or intensity? Can we better see how Christian friendship relates to the views, and the wisdom, of the ancient thinkers?

Answers to these questions are at hand, thanks to a third theologian to whom we will now turn. He does not tower among the theologians of the West; he was merely a monk-administrator who lived about a hundred years before Aquinas. But he wrote a short book (comprising three short dialogues) on precisely this question. While Aquinas opens up how to think about friendship and love with respect to God, this monk spells out the resolution of the Christian quandary of love and friendship with other people.

Aelred of Rievaulx: Understanding Friendship Christianly

As friendship is an implicit theme running through the life of Augustine, it is an explicit theme running through the life of Aelred of Rievaulx (c. 1110–67). Coming from a line of married priests in the north of England, Aelred was sent, around the age of fifteen, to serve in the court of Scotland's king, forming there "close friendships" with the king's heir and stepsons. His character seems to have been disposed at once to friendship and to a desire for holiness as a Christian. In time, he chose to leave the court, later reflecting that the pleasure of "the welcome attachment of friendship" did not persist in that environment but rather inevitably declined: "I contemplated the happiness we felt at the beginning of those friendships; I considered their progress; I foresaw their end." That progress was growing fear of giving offense, and that end was recrimination.[9] So in 1134, he joined the Cistercians in Rievaulx, where he had discovered a community of Christian love, and there he would work out how friendship and Christian love are related to each other. In 1143, he left Rievaulx to become the first abbot of a daughter house, but he returned after a few years to be abbot at Rievaulx itself. This proved strenuous work; his health was failing by 1157, when his duties were lightened; he continued there to his death.

Like Augustine's, Aelred's life involved considerable "administration" (as we would say), but unlike Augustine's, his health was weakened and his life not as extended (about fifty-seven years to Augustine's seventy-six). His written work is but a fraction of that of the African bishop, and even what he did write was sometimes less than enthusiastically received. Despite all these obstacles, he manages in his work *Spiritual Friendship* to show the way to solve the problem of friendship, not only theologically but also practically.

Spiritual Friendship is a short work in three books, one book for each dialogue. His interlocutor in the first book seems to have died before the conversation of book II takes place; one assumes the intervention of a number of years (either there was a delay in composition or Aelred sets it up thus as a literary device). Books II and III have two new interlocutors and take place on successive days. In each book, there is a sense that the conversation occurs in scarce time stolen away from work, conversation welcome in its own right, precious and yet limited. When the hour (if it was an hour) was up, the dialogue had to be ended.

Mark Williams, a Protestant scholar at Calvin University who has given us a fresh translation of *Spiritual Friendship*, reminds us, as we have seen in Aristotle and Cicero, that "in both antiquity and the middle ages, it was difficult to begin a friendship": people of those times had a high view of friendship, and they expected much of their friends.[10] In this, they were quite different from us moderns, who speak casually of taking up friends and did so even before the "face book" was a gleam in Mark Zuckerberg's eyes. When I went to seminary (which was after the invention of the light bulb but before "Facebook"), the deli owner just down the street was friendly with all of us seminarians and our families. He greeted each of us cordially as "friend"—but not by name. It seems harsh to say the truth that, friendly as he was, we were not in fact friends. We moderns don't want to make sharp judgments of that sort; we fear appearing to be unfriendly. By contrast, the ancients and the people of Aelred's time would have had no problem denying that a casual acquaintance was a friend.

This difficulty of forming friendships is an early topic of the first book, a dialogue between Aelred and his "dearest friend," Ivo. In his first sentence, Aelred intimates that any existing friendship is a gift in Christ: "Here we are, you and I, and I hope that Christ makes a third with us." Aelred, having sensed that Ivo is burdened, invites him to "reveal your heart and speak your mind" in this special, private time of "opportunity and leisure" (I.1).[11] He also points out that their friendship is based on the good, that Ivo doesn't get involved with empty talk but is "always engaged in some beneficial pursuit" for his "spiritual development," and that their friendship has mutuality in which they each "learn and teach, give and receive" (I.4)—this despite their difference in age and status (as Ivo tries briefly to object). So far, so classical.

But what difference does Christ make to friendship? Ivo, whose friendship with Aelred has been quickly established as classical, seeks to understand friendship as a Christian. What is Christian friendship—which is what Aelred means by "spiritual friendship"? Where does it come from? What is it for? Is it for everyone? And can it continue through a life unbroken?

Aelred commends Cicero, who has written well on friendship, but Ivo is suspicious. Cicero, he points out, does not know "the honey-sweet name of Christ," which has claimed Ivo's affections (I.7). Ivo wants "our most common assumptions about friendship" to be "proved by the authority of scripture" (I.8). Aelred agrees to take up the task.

He takes the Ciceronian definition of friendship and gives it a Christian interpretation. "Friendship," Cicero says in his classic definition (which we also saw earlier), "is agreement on both human and divine affairs, combined with good will and mutual esteem" (I.11). Aelred takes "good will" as "the mental emotion of friendship," and "mutual esteem" as "the expression of friendship in deeds" (I.15). Friendship itself Aelred interprets (conventionally, as does Cicero) from its root in *amor* (love): *amicus* (friend) comes from love, and *amicitia* (friendship) likewise follows. Love, he goes on, is "an affection of the rational mind" that "seeks something for itself with desire and strives to enjoy" it, and to enjoy it internally as well, and to preserve it (I.19). A friend is "the guardian of love," or better, "my friend must be the guardian of our mutual love, or even of my very soul." This points to the good, indeed the ultimate good, that is the point of friendship. To do this, the friend must be able to keep secrets and also appropriately correct flaws in the friend or endure them. "When I rejoice, he will rejoice; when I grieve, he will grieve with me; he will consider as his own everything that his friend experiences" (I.20). Again, very classical: friends have all things in common. Yet we whiff the scriptural aroma ("Rejoice with them that do rejoice, and weep with them that weep" [Rom. 12:15]).

The philosophers, Aelred says, agree with this, as does the wisdom literature of the Bible. He quotes Proverbs 17:17, "He who is a friend loves for all time" (I.21), which "makes it quite clear that friendship is eternal, provided it is true friendship." Aelred takes this verse from Proverbs to mean that if a friendship ends, it was never really a friendship. (The whole verse, "A friend loveth at all times, and a brother is born for adversity," suggests that while siblings are particularly important in times of adversity, a friend will love us in all the various times of our life.) Even if one "is nailed to the cross, 'he who is a friend loves for all time'" (I.23)—which is rather more than a whiff of Scripture. Aelred (if I may put it so) nails pagan friendship, with its desire to endure without end, to the friendship accomplished on the cross for all time.

Is the Number of Friends Small?

But Ivo, still not satisfied, brings forth the pessimistic view common to the ancients and his contemporaries. If friendship is so hard, it necessarily will be rare. And if friendship is rare, he is unlikely to find what he wants; he despairs of achieving friendship himself. Aelred tells him—it is a gentle rebuke, the sort of correction that a friend offers a friend—that even if friendship were rare, he must not despair of achieving it. No Christian should lack hope of attaining any virtue; indeed, our Lord said, "Seek, and ye shall find" (Matt. 7:7). Then he gives reason.

The ancients, not knowing Christ, did not know that he is the one who dispenses virtues. (Aelred quotes Ps. 24:10, but instead of "The Lord of hosts," he reads, "*The Lord of virtues* himself is the King of glory" [I.27, emphasis added]). And that means, says Aelred, that he will not speak "of merely three or four pairs of friends, as the pagans do, but I set before you a thousand pairs of friends, who by faith in the Lord were ready to die one for another—in short, to do as a matter of course what the pagans said or imagined a great miracle in the case of Pylades and Orestes" (I.28). We noted earlier Cicero's reference to a then-recent play in which Orestes was to be put to death, and Pylades and Orestes each stepped forward, saying, "I am Orestes," because they were such close friends that each wanted to die instead of the other. Well, Aelred says, Jesus Christ, the Lord of all the virtues, gives friendship to many. There have been thousands of Christian martyrs willing to die, who have in fact died, for their friends—indeed, not just thousands but a countless host. Jesus, he says, speaking through the Psalms, "foretold these martyrs; he spoke, 'and they were multiplied beyond number'" (I.30; cf. Ps. 40:5). Jesus has multiplied friends beyond all counting, for of course, although Jesus' friends are willing to die for each other, only some have martyrdom thrust upon them. Which is to say that the vast number of martyrs testifies to the even vaster extent of the spread—the massive explosion—of friendship within Christianity. Aelred clinches his argument with John 15:13: "Greater love hath no man than this, that a man lay down his life for his friends." Clearly, for Aelred, Jesus' declaration is the key to the interpretation of all human friendship, and particularly the key to the magnificent and, to an ancient mindset, incredible multiplication of friendship among the followers of Jesus.

How Friendship and Christian Love Are the Same and Yet Different

Aelred ultimately interprets friendship as, in God's design, the same as Christian love. In God's design, *agape* is *philia*, *caritas* is *amicitia*. But until the consequences of the fall are overcome, friendship and

Christian love will have a certain separation. On the one hand, there is the universal love that we owe to all people, even our enemies. On the other hand, friendship is reserved for a few with whom we have a reciprocal sharing of love that is based on the good. Aelred therefore gives a genealogical account, a narrative, within which we can place the classical (Ciceronian/Aristotelian) teaching about friendship and affirm it, while through the narrative we can overcome what the moral theologian Oliver O'Donovan has rightly identified as the "sense of tragedy" that "hangs over the classical discourse of friendship."[12]

Here is Aelred's account of how this separation came about. First, we see that everything is created by God and shows God's purpose for "all his creatures to be joined together in peace, and for community to exist between them." With a sensitivity that we could well identify as "ecological," Aelred says that there is nothing in creation that is left alone by itself. Rather, God has linked everything "together in a certain community out of diversity" (I.53). His argument runs from stones to trees and plants and even to angels. Angels, one might think, would pose a problem for him, since, as is traditional, he holds that there is only one angel per angelic species. Take something that is not angelic—may I pick on cats again? The reason we have many cats, the reason why we have many individuals of any given species, is because of physical matter; matter is what differentiates individuals within a species. Angels, however, being pure spirits, have no matter, and thus they are singular: one angel, one species. Yet Aelred sees God's desire for creaturely fellowship even here: "Even among the angels divine wisdom saw to it that not just one, but many were created, among whom community was welcome and the sweetest love created a unity of will and affection." The unity of the angels is given prior to the recognition of difference in rank (the hierarchy of angelic species) so that the angelic hierarchy "would be no occasion for envy—but the joy of friendship. . . . And so sheer numbers banished solitude, and mutual participation in joy increased the happiness of the many" (I.56).

But for humans, we are a single species—descended from, according to the biblical narrative, a single pair of parents. It is thus essential for the man and the woman of Genesis 2 to be equal with each other if they are to be friends. Hence, Aelred rejoices in both the creation of the woman and the manner of her creation: "Woman was created expressly as an incentive for happiness and friendship, from the very substance of the man himself. And so it is beautiful that the second created being was taken from the side of the first, so that nature might teach that all are equals, as it were 'collateral.' In human affairs there is to be neither superior nor inferior; this is the appropriate mark of friendship" (I.57). As Williams notes, Aelred makes a Latin pun here: the woman comes from the *latus*, the side, of the man, and thus they are *collateral*, brought together in a side-by-side equality.[13]

The Fall from Friendship

Let us turn from Aelred for a moment to consider his claim of aboriginal human equality, for there is wisdom buried in Genesis 2 and 3, wisdom waiting for a careful reader but easy to pass by.

First, we should note the rather strong claim that the "good and evil" of the forbidden tree can indicate knowledge of a political character, and in particular, the wisdom that a ruler needs to have. Following the principle of allowing the Bible to interpret itself, we will find the same Hebrew words used in Solomon's prayer asking God for what he needs to be a good king: "an understanding heart to judge thy people, that I may discern between good and bad" (1 Kings 3:9). The knowledge of "good and bad" (elsewhere translated as the knowledge of "good and evil") is here explicitly linked with the discernments, the judgments, that a ruler must make. It is the knowledge that a king needs to have.[14]

This insight can then illuminate the overall trajectory of Genesis 2. The human enters the scene as a lowly creature whose job is to bring the seeds that are in the earth to fruition (v. 5). But it seems he is discovered to have more dignity than that, and so a garden is made for him (v. 8). Then, just as God is about to bring to awareness that it is not good for him to be alone, God tells him not to eat of the tree of political knowledge (vv. 17–18). God does not want him to know about ruling. To be innocent of knowledge of ruling seems to be necessary for God to create an equal for him, a fitting "help-meet": God does not want there to be rule or governance (with its resulting inequalities) between the human and his companion. Only with this prohibition in place does God make the animals. Presumably, one of them might have been found to be the human's equal companion, but in the event, none of them was fitting (vv. 19–20). Finally, God causes "a deep sleep to fall upon" the human, and from his side the woman is taken (vv. 21–22), in the implicit equality of friendship that Aelred celebrates.

It follows that their subsequent eating from the forbidden tree is the eruption of the world of politics into their existence. This is a world of superiors and inferiors, a world of command and obedience. This world of power dynamics is what underlies God's pronouncements of the consequences of their acquisition of this sort of knowledge. There is "enmity" between one creature, at least, and the humans (Gen. 3:15). There is "sorrow" in childbearing (we will suggest this includes a self-awareness of mortality); there is "desire" for the husband, who "shall rule" over his wife (v. 16). And to complete the circle, the man, expelled from the garden, is returned to his initial humble place as one whose job is to bring seeds to fruition, now with his own "sorrow" at the time of eating—"in sorrow shalt thou eat of [the ground] all the days of thy life" (v. 17). Communion at table has become a time of sorrow rather than one of fellowship, of happiness—of friendship.

Enmity of one with another, rule of one over another, sorrow rather than friendship—these details of our primal narrative are clearly congruent with Aelred's understanding of an aboriginal divine purpose to make creation an arena of universal friendship and fellowship. The divine purpose was for this fellowship to flourish in the very high form of friendship in the human species. The fall is precisely deviation from this purpose, and its consequence the loss of universal human friendship. Aboriginal human nature, according to Aelred, gave people "the emotional desire for friendship and affection," which was increased by the experience of its "sweetness" (I.58). But the fall brought corruption and division. As a result, "those who were good began to distinguish between affection and friendship." They saw that affection should be given to all people, even "those who are enemies and perverse," but the "fellowship of wills [and] counsel," which is of the essence of friendship, had to be reserved for the good (I.59).

And with regard to politics, Aelred, despite giving it scant attention, does claim that human law became necessary after the fall to regulate friendship and put it in order. The law is needed, he says, to distinguish carnal and worldly (so-called) friendships from "true friendship." The necessity of the law, it seems, pertains to the law's educative function: by whatever regulatory method (and Aelred is entirely unspecific on this), the law would save people who were looking for true friendship from being "caught unawares" in one of the false forms; the law would point out that despite their similarities, carnal and worldly "friendships" are not authentic friendship (I.61).

The Bible, of course, has much more to say about politics than that its origin is in the failure of friendship. Robert Sacks finds, for instance, a suggestion that the sacrificial system, which is established as an important part of the government of Israel, aims at the restoration of human communion.[15] A Christian might find further positive appreciation of political authority in Jesus, ascended and reigning from God's right hand. But Aelred, who left the court of an earthly king in order to enter a monastery, surely has a right understanding of the fundamentals: we were made for universal friendship, and that has been lost.

Real Friendship Is Spiritual Friendship

Yet although universal friendship has been lost, we have not lost altogether the innate human longing to have friends. So we have the lesser relationships, the false forms and simulacra that trade off the real thing. Aelred denominates as "carnal" friendship a bond between people who are in agreement about vices. And "worldly" friendship is what he calls a relationship from which each hopes to profit. These have "the mere name" of friendship; each such relationship "looks like friendship," but only spiritual friendship is truly so. In a spiritual friendship, people are bound together by having similar good character, goals, and habits (I.36–38). These distinctions correlate well with Aristotle's differentiation of friendships as based on the pleasant, the useful, and the good.

On this side of the fall, Christians have, in effect, a double calling. They are to love all people, to have *caritas* for all, the word for Christian love that of old would have been translated "charity" but Williams takes variously as "good will" and "grace."[16] One wants to manifest grace to one's neighbor, to have goodwill toward all people. And yet one cannot share one's heart and mind but with a few people—and they need to be people who can reciprocate that sharing. Such a spiritual commonality, a communion involving character, goals, and habits, is emotionally packed in a way that *caritas* is not, *precisely because it is shared*. We remember Aristotle saying that to share with a friend is the pleasantest thing human beings can enjoy. Aelred would agree: spiritual friendship is enjoyable. And it is not a cause for guilt, as if one were wrongly holding back from offering friendship to others.

The reason for calling true friendship "spiritual" is made clearer in books II and III, which are set, as we noted above, some time after the first book and involve two new interlocutors, Walter and Gratian. Friendship, Aelred tells them, "is a path to the love and knowledge of God." Its "special token" is the feeling of pleasure, security, sweetness, and delight that friends share in all things. Thus "from the perfection of Christian love, we are able to esteem those who are otherwise burdensome or unpleasant to us; we take account of their interests honestly, not disingenuously, not deceitfully, but truly and without being compelled to do so. However, we do not admit them to the privacy of our friendship" (II.18–19).

Friendship is always love, but love in this fallen world is not always friendship, and therein lies the need for care in the selection of one's friends. Spiritual friendship needs a "solid foundation," and that is nothing other than "the love of God" (III.5). This time when Aelred repeats Cicero's definition (which in the first book he quoted to Ivo), he adds, as O'Donovan has noted,[17] an adjective: friendship is "the *highest* agreement on both human and divine affairs, combined with good will and mutual esteem" (III.8, emphasis added). Here Aelred subtly reveals his answer to the question, What is the good which is the point of true friendship? It is "the highest agreement," combined with affection and love, on all things. And that highest agreement has its solid foundation in the *caritas* of God, his gift of grace, the love that is God's own being that he gives to us.

Aelred helps us grasp the specificity of spiritual friendship. It includes love (*dilectio*), "a show of favor that proceeds from benevolence." It also involves affection (*affectio*), that "certain inner pleasure [that] comes from friendship." Moreover, friendship provides an environment of security (*securitas*, reassurance) within which one may reveal "all one's secrets and purposes without fear or suspicion." And finally, it has delight (*jucunditas*) at the experience of minds meeting each other in "an agreement that is pleasant and benevolent—concerning all matters, whether happy or sad, which have a bearing on the friendship, everything that we teach or learn" (III.51). Showing love for each other, with its particular pleasure, a safe place to share all of one's heart, with the delight that comes from agreement on the highest things—this is what spiritual friendship looks like.

And it remains supremely satisfying for human beings. We humans long for "that great and wondrous happiness" that we have when "God himself is at work and pouring forth such great friendship and love between himself and his creation," which leads to each loving the other as he loves himself. "And through this friendship each one rejoices in the happiness of another as much as in his own; and so the happiness of individuals is the happiness of all, and the universality of the happiness of all becomes the happiness of individuals." When this comes to be, "there is no concealment of thoughts, no dissimulation of affection." Such "true and eternal friendship . . . takes shape here, in this world, and is perfected in the next; here it is the property of the few who are good; there, where all are good, it is the property of all" (III.79–80).

Aelred has more teaching than what I summarize here: how to choose friends, whether friendship should ever be broken off, and what to do when one's friend falls short. Some of these practical matters (along with others) will concern us later on. But for now, here in the middle of this book, it is fitting for us to pause to give thanks for Aelred's exposition of friendship as the consummation of Christian life and hope's promise.

EIGHT

Unapologetic Celibacy

The Original Human, Sex, and Friendship

This chapter is the hardest one of this book. Patient reader, we have thought with some of the smartest people of human history about the important matter of friendship. We have seen that there are good reasons to hold that friendship is the point of being human, that our ultimate happiness is found in friendship, and that, for Christians, this desire for friendship extends ever more broadly and includes even friendship with God. All this is highly countercultural, but it is as nothing compared to our next topic.

What shall we say about sex?

We return to Genesis 2, which Aelred showed us is about the establishment of friendship, to attend now to a rather obvious detail. There are two human beings; one is male and one is female. What is the significance of sexual difference? How does it relate to friendship?

We retrace the logic of Genesis 2 with sex in mind. God pronounced that it was not good for the human to be alone. This spurred the creation of the beasts of the field and the fowls of the air. It seems their creation was prepared for by the preceding injunction for the human to avoid political knowledge, the knowledge of "good and bad" that Solomon, much later, prays for in order that he might rule Israel well. The suggestion is that the resulting community of humans and birds and beasts was to be egalitarian, without rule or lawmaking or the relation of command and obedience. Yet birds and beasts, although capable of meaningful community with the human, were not able to remove the problem of his aloneness.

The original human, discovered to be lacking in his aloneness, needed a friend. As it turned out, true friendship waited upon the emergence of the woman from the side of the man.

This, one hardly needs to say, is not a historical account; the promise, however, is that if we attend closely to the Word of God as written, we can find therein depths of mystery. So it is here with the original human being. Traditionally translated as "man" and given a masculine pronoun, "he" might be pictured in our minds with male sexual apparatus; when woman is made out of his side, then (in this imagining) the original singular male comes to have a complement. Yet it seems to me that the text is patient of another reading. The "man" that God made from the dust of the earth could have been (for all the difference it makes in the story) a being without gender, sexless. And then when the help-meet for "him," "his" fitting companion, comes into being from "his" side, both sexes are created at once. "He" awakes from sleep as male, and she who stands before him is female.

This reading interestingly deprioritizes the male, but more importantly, it coheres with the teaching of the rest of the chapter: that the primal garden was to be a place of communion without rule. Yet whether we imagine the original singular human as being a male or not, the story teaches us that friendship makes its appearance and becomes a concrete human possibility precisely when there is another human being who is, as a woman at the side of a man, at once the same and yet irreducibly different. A human and a bird, or a human and a beast, whatever fellowship they may have, are found in this story not to be similar enough for friendship. Equality of a fundamental sort is needed.

Still, although needed, fundamental equality is not enough. At the point when friendship emerges as a possibility—the point where there are two human beings—the text shows the two as non-interchangeable, visibly different and inescapably so. One can see them as exactly equal: neither was there prior to the other, for the original human somehow contained the woman that God fashioned from that original human's side. They are exactly equal, and yet they cannot be interchanged, a point guaranteed by their sexual difference. The friendship that answers the problem of human aloneness is made with one who is equal (in a way that no other creature is equal) and yet different in a manner that perdures.

Now the text immediately comments that their sexual difference is the origin of marriage. And in the way the story continues through the acquisition of the knowledge of good and bad, the expulsion from the garden, the giving of the law, and so forth, this story does give an account of the origin of marriage. The point, in fact, is made by the text itself. The two emerge as a separation made out of the original human; there is delight in their meet-ness, their fittingness for each other, and thus, it says, "shall a man leave his father and his mother, and shall cleave unto his wife: and they shall be one flesh" (Gen. 2:24). That this verse is significant for our understanding of marriage is underlined by Jesus' singling it out in his teaching on divorce (e.g., Matt. 19:5). So the reader cannot deny that Genesis 2 is about marriage. Was Aelred wrong, are we wrong, if we persist in seeing it as pointing to the origin also, and perhaps even more so, of friendship?

We may find our first clue if we ask where those words "his father and his mother" came from, there in the garden. In the garden, those words cannot refer to anything: there are only two human beings, neither having the history marked by a belly button. No mothers and no fathers are in this picture; the text does not itself give any referent or contextual meaning for such terms. The verse about a man leaving his parents provides an explanation of something that comes after the garden: it explains the function (or one function) of sexual difference in our world after the fall. It is, in the context of the story, a parenthetical remark, an aside spoken to the reader. For us, a man and a woman who leave their childhood homes and form together a new thing—"one flesh"—are creating new and successive generations. One generation follows upon another; the new comes, the old passes away. Such is the place of marriage in our world: the constitutive link of the generations, the divinely given means for new families to arise as the older ones die off.

But we are not required to hold that the postlapsarian context of fathers and mothers and children had to be the original, prelapsarian point of sexual difference.

This brings our attention to another feature of Genesis 2. In this chapter, there is only one instance of every animal and bird, and there are only two human beings. There is no command to any of them to be fruitful and multiply and fill the spaces God has made for them. Genesis 1, by contrast, is trying to show the importance of sexual difference as the means of being fruitful and completing the plenitude of the creation God has made. Genesis 2 has a subtly different and complementary emphasis. It focuses on the problem of aloneness. That problem is solved once there are two humans, one male, one female. Once the problem is solved, there need not be any more.

We may note that the text does not specify what "male" and "female" mean in the garden, nor does it interpret their "cleaving" for us. To cleave to each other seems to have been their spontaneous joy, a sexual embrace that put the two back together. Not only has the one been made two, but the two are also one. But what was the character of that sexual embrace? Most early Christian theologians (with Augustine as a notable exception) thought there would have been no children had there been no fall. And that means two people, only two people, living forever. (It seems also to mean one cat, one dog, one horse, one swallow, and so forth.) Which is to say, the two humans would live forever, without aging or death or succeeding generations, thanks to that tree of life, the named but not forbidden tree. And in that case, the question of the relationship of sex and friendship would never arise. The man and the woman, solitary apart but not solitary together, would have cleaved to each other, and they would have been friends. Our problem—how to recover friendship in our day and the problem of the place of sex within friendship—would never have become their problem.

We should note that even for Augustine, who held that sexual relations in the garden would have been procreative, the purpose of God in creating human beings was for them to have friendship. That is to say, for Augustine, friendship is more fundamental than marriage in God's design. "Since every man is a part of the human race, and human nature is something social and possesses the capacity for friendship as a great and natural good, for this reason God wished to create all men from one." Endowed thus at creation, we have a built-in capacity for friendship, a "great and natural good." Indeed, for Augustine, the point of marriage is friendship. Marriage is a "natural companionship between the two sexes"; quite apart from procreation or sexual intercourse, "the marriage of male and female is something good."[1]

In this part of Genesis, there is a further depth—namely, the absence of vulnerability in the garden. One of each animal is enough because no animal dies. There is no ruling of one over another but only the friendly fellowship of the beasts with the man and the woman, themselves cleaving to each other in invulnerable friendship. This "cleaving" of the original man and woman does not—as the next verse points out—entail or result in the knowledge of nakedness, a knowledge that comes to be after the fall and is connected with shame (contrast Gen. 2:25 with 3:7). To know you are naked is to know you are vulnerable.

The ultimate vulnerability, which clothing may cause us to forget but cannot overcome, is the vulnerability to death. God had told the original human, when he forbade eating the fruit of the tree of political knowledge, that "in the day that thou eatest thereof thou shalt surely die" (Gen. 2:17). But he did not forbid eating of the other named tree, the tree of life (2:9), and once the humans took on political knowledge, he found it necessary to expedite their expulsion from the garden lest they eat of it also and thus have unending life as political beings subject to rule and obedience and sorrow (3:22–23). Thus it appears that the mortality that comes from political knowledge is neither instant nor inevitable death. Having become mortal by their own shameful disobedience, they understand their genitals not as shameful in themselves but as the mark of their shame. Fallen, they have become procreators. The mark of their shame will be their children—a paradoxical mark, to be sure, since bearing and rearing children will also be a mark of their hope.

In Genesis 2 and 3 there is no "knowledge" of nakedness that is not shame filled. Robert Sacks, whose work on Job and Genesis we noted earlier, asks, "Why should nakedness be shameful outside the Garden and yet not shameful within?" One reason, he puts forth, is that the most painful thing in human life—more painful than all our other "pains and labors"—is our knowledge that we will die, that our life will come to an end. "But the act of procreation is intended to be a replacement for immortality and hence a constant reminder to man of his mortality. Since sexual relations in the Garden did not have that character," he concludes, "there was no reason for shame."[2]

We have been focusing on Genesis 2, the so-called second creation account of the Bible, for the reason that it addresses the problem of solitude and thus has promise for insight into human friendship. By having complementary creation accounts, the Bible suggests that there will be no simple answer to any question about our human origins. The first chapter gives us a glorious cosmic vision of creation as a whole, opening with the great expanses of air and water that God initially brings into being, which he then, in days four, five, and six, fills with creatures who, with his blessing, assist in the completion of creation's fullness. The fish are to fill the water and the birds the air, and to human beings is given the earth. "Be fruitful, and multiply, and fill . . . the earth" (Gen. 1:22; cf. 1:28). Genesis 1 does not face the problem of human aloneness but simply assumes its solution by creating humans, along with everything else, in plurality. It is a creation account of abundance and indeed plenitude, with a blessing to fruitfulness and multiplication and filling—and, significantly, no fall (although it has hints of it: "rule" and "dominion" appear, unanticipated, in vv. 16, 26, and 28). In the very different account that begins in Genesis 2, fallen humanity knows it is fallen because it is mortal; the sign of its mortality is that it has children, children who attest to the hope in the hearts of their parents even as their arrival on the stage foreshadows their parents' exit.

Genesis 2 is a close-framed creation account. It has no spaces that need to be filled; the garden needs only to be tended. It is designed as a place of equality and friendship, without rule and, at least to explicit appearance, without procreation. Disobedient man and woman, exiled into a harsh world of rule and obedience and sorrow, will know they are—beneath whatever protection their clothing may allow—naked. However much they cover up the fact, they are exposed to a hostile or indifferent world in which they will die, and human life will continue not in themselves but in the succession of their descendants, who will gradually spread abroad over the difficult soil of earth. There is (there has to be!) a role for friendship in this world—a centrally important role and a precious one, as the vulnerable Job came to see.

What might this mean about the relation of sex and friendship?

Experiencing Sex and Being Human

For clarity, let's put it baldly. One must have friends in order to be fully human. One need not marry or otherwise have sexual intercourse in order to be fully human.

This is why I have labored to show that friendship is the inner meaning of Genesis 2: as Aelred says, "Woman was created expressly as an incentive for happiness and friendship" (I.57).[3] For us who are fallen, Genesis 2 is also a story of the origin of marriage, but its deeper purpose is to reveal friendship as the point of human plurality.

But what will we then say about our friendships? Should we seek somehow to go back to paradise, to restore somehow our original goodness? No. The text makes it clear that the garden is not for us, and we are not to seek to return to it. Redemption in Christ is no restoration to the original paradise; it is something new, encompassing both vulnerability and rule. Christ's nakedness on the cross shows his complete human vulnerability. And there, as the king of all kings, he opens for us not a politics-free zone, not a primitive, egalitarian garden—but a kingdom.

Is there a place for sexual relations in the kingdom? Jesus teaches—it is the insight with which we began—that in the kingdom of God, there is no marriage. This teaching signals that the "cleaving" of the garden, at least if it is interpreted as sexual union, is not characteristic of redeemed humanity. It seems to me that a more intense intimacy is on offer to those who seek the kingdom. But at any rate, we should welcome these questions because—although I have called it, conventionally, "the fall"—the disobedience of the two humans in the garden had many joyful results. Adam indeed seems from the start to be a fundamentally hopeful man, for immediately after God pronounces the dire consequences for the humans and the animals and the earth,

Adam calls the woman Eve to signify that she is the mother of all the living. It is as if he were saying, "Life is going to be hard; we are all going to have to endure rule and obedience and pain and toil—but, goodness, how many people there are going to be!" That is the mark of a hopeful soul. If what happened in the garden was a fall, it was nonetheless *felix culpa*, a happy fall. We can rejoice that now the population of the kingdom of heaven can be huge, and that means that the possibilities for friendship in the end may reach beyond all number.

The Sex Question and Jesus

Jesus taught that there is no marriage in the kingdom of heaven. The resurrected body is to be deathless without decay of any sort. There will be no disease, no aging—and thus no children growing into adulthood.[4] In this sense, it will be like the original paradise: there won't be generations, for in the world to come, people will not progress through various stages of life.

We should contemplate the universal friendship of the kingdom of God without wondering whether there will be multiple if not universal paired-up cleavings. Jesus' teaching (that he has come to reestablish friendship, that the kingdom has no giving and taking in marriage) shows us that in the end the cleaving of marriage is incompatible with the universal friendship of the kingdom of God; it will pass away, but friendship will endure. But we are not there yet. In this life, which includes the eschatological call to have and be friends, some of us, some of the time, experience the particular form of friendship that is marriage. For us, friendship and the sexual embrace are not mutually exclusive; indeed, the cleaving of marriage can be experienced as a heightened measure of intimacy that goes beyond other experience. Despite this, there remains in this life a stark difference between the exclusivity of marriage (leaving father and mother, and indeed all others, for this spouse) and the innate expansiveness of the desire for friendship, where one may be added without leaving others behind.

These are theological clues that invite us to imagine something rarely thought of: an intimacy with friends that is deep, like that experienced by lovers but not expressed or prepared for by an intimate physical cleaving. This intimacy, since it is not physically consummated, is open to new friends in a way that marriage is closed. And even more speculatively, might these same clues also invite us to imagine that in the world to come there is some sort of nonsexual "cleaving" that pertains to the profound intimacy of friends? Could that be the complete mutual understanding that Jesus gives in his flesh and blood?

These reflections, these speculations, these guesses—they all hang on a willingness to say something that many people will find offensive. Dear reader, how Christianly countercultural are you willing to be? I take no pleasure in multiplying grounds of offense, and so this is not a point I have trumpeted in sermons or teaching or writing. It is with some repentance, therefore, that I say we need to make this clear: one need not experience sexual union in order to experience the fullness of being human. Saying this will be received as scandal, and yet it may be that *this* is the particular proclamation we Christians today are called upon to make unabashedly.

Consider again the life of Jesus. He, according to all reliable testimony, did not experience sexual relations. Yet despite this, faith attests him as the one complete human being. (Being without sin means he had nothing that subtracted from his humanity; we must keep in mind that the essence of sin is a failure to be fully human.) To be faithful to the revelation in Jesus, we must say that the experience of sexual union is not needed for a full and complete human life.

There is no reason to belabor how radically this runs against the thought patterns and assumed truths of our age. Sex, we are told a thousand times a day, is natural; to abstain from it is unnatural and creepy. The film *The 40-Year-Old Virgin*, for instance, plays on this assumption (while also here and there savvily undermining it). There are shows called *The Bachelor* and *The Bachelorette*, I am told, which trade on the same assumption. Sex is a normal thing that consenting adults do; it's just a part of being human.

A widow gave me a recent memoir that had been given to her, *The Widower's Notebook*, with a note for me to pass it on, read or unread. It's the sort of book many well-intentioned people give to those whose spouses have died. (My own *Losing Susan* probably falls into the same category.) The author, a writer and artist, and his wife, similarly creative, had been married for forty years. Then a simple meniscus surgery quickly led to her death, possibly through medical malpractice (a combination of medicines felled her within days). He writes grippingly, starting there at the end and moving backward and forward, filling the reader in with details of their life together and chronicling his ongoing, now single life. Very soon people start asking him to go out. He isn't ready. They invite him to dinner parties; he puts them off. His conversations with his friends reveal asymmetric assumptions: they are certain he needs to find another woman, or at least have sex. Not a friend or acquaintance in the book assumes otherwise. He himself dismisses celibacy as his future, but he wants more time, feels pushed. He knows that having sex with a friend would change the friendship forever, perhaps detrimentally, so it isn't going to be a casual step for him. One friend, finally, gets him to meet her for dinner. He is late; he starts to apologize. She asks him to guess what she has been doing. He says, "Waiting." She says she has been making a list of what she needs to do. "One: have sex. Two: go away for a romantic weekend and have more sex. Three . . ."[5] After dinner they walk and stop in a bar for drinks. They walk to her home; she asks him if he wants to come up for coffee—he recalls, in *Seinfeld*, how the question about coffee is always a euphemism for sex. He says no.

Sometime later, after a buddy invites him into an exclusive online prostitute service (he declines), after a couple have him over for dinner (he declines their offer to introduce him to a suitable and sexy woman; the wife says never mind, he'll be f***ing her or someone else soon enough), and after many other such conversations, a young woman comes up to him at a party. She is half his age and turns out to have been a student of his several years ago. They get talking, they go out for a walk, she invites him to her place. They have sex, several times, over what we gather is a few months. But they are clearly unequal: he never invites her to his place, for instance; their interests are quite different; they don't share much besides sex. It wasn't what he wanted. What he wanted, of course, was for his wife to be alive.

It is a sex-saturated world out there, but some people would be open to hearing from the church that an alternative exists, something that is not negative (focusing on what you are not doing—namely, not having sex) but, to the contrary, positive (what you are doing—namely, building real intimacy in friendship). Here Christianity could be countercultural in a big way. But we need to be so wisely, with simultaneous cunning and innocence. (As Matthew has Jesus say, "Behold, I send you forth as sheep in the midst of wolves: be ye therefore wise as serpents, and harmless as doves" [10:16].) We need to listen to people, to find out what they really think, and we need to attend to social science data. The late-modern, laissez-faire sexual landscape is not empowering people to flourish. It does not satisfy the human longing for friendship, which is what human beings are made for. It is a gospel opening.

Celibacy Is for Everybody

Traditional Christian teaching about the place for sexual relations is clear: sexual relations belong in marriage and nowhere else. The explanations for this have varied, and the ranking of marriage vis-à-vis, for instance, vowed celibacy has also varied. But sex outside of marriage has, at best, been tolerated as a concession to a fallen world, and in this, Christianity has found itself hugely countercultural, not least in the environment of late antiquity in which it emerged.

This teaching means that Christianity calls every person, without exception, to celibacy for at least part of his or her life. We are called to be celibate prior to marriage. We are expected to be chaste if we marry, which means many things but includes having sexual relations with none save our spouse. And if our spouse dies, we are to return to celibacy, which continues for the rest of our life unless we marry again. Moreover, Christianity also has no expectation that any given person will marry or should marry or should seek to marry. So its clear teaching is that celibacy is for everybody, at least for part of life and sometimes for all of it. And furthermore—by the logic of this teaching, if not in the actual experience of people in congregations—this is a good and natural thing. It is not unnatural to be unmarried and therefore celibate—not unnatural and not harmful in itself.

So far so clear. Difficulties come in explanations, for to explain is to put a teaching in a particular cultural context, whereas this teaching extends universally.

Christian teaching can affirm that sexual relations are capable of ecstasy, a powerful pleasure that takes one out of oneself and can bind one particularly close to one's sexual partner. (In a hook-up culture, this sexual affirmation is already countercultural.) Sexual ecstasy is in a sense sacramental: it points to the joy of total, mutual self-giving. Of course, there is much tawdry sex and much rather everyday sex, but its binding force is there and is a unique pleasure.

Yet to say that sex is a powerful pleasure, or even a unique pleasure, is not to say that it is a necessary human experience. There are other extraordinary and intense pleasurable experiences of ecstatic magnitude. Skydiving is said to be one, as are acid trips, and even, as happened to Dostoyevsky, being blindfolded and bound for execution, hearing the rifles go off, and finding one is still alive. A sensitive and accomplished artist can show us how these other intense experiences may contain their own erotic element or even be compared to a sexual climax. In the emergency room for back pain, I felt the narcotic enter my lower right arm. It went up to my shoulder, crossed my chest, then eased down through my whole body. While I did not experience arousal, I could understand if someone were to compare a drug experience with a postcoital sense of well-being. It was a bliss I had never experienced before and have not had since.

Pleasure is good in itself, and great pleasures are to be particularly valued, for they are signs of the goodness of God. The best pleasures are shared. Yet it is not necessary to our human flourishing that we have any of them in particular. The traditional Christian teaching is that the goodness of sexual union lies in marriage, but one who does not experience this good has no more a diminishment of human flourishing than a person who never jumps out of an airplane.

To speak broadly, all pleasures should be understood as ways of binding people together; sexual congress is something like an archetype for this. It is vividly, literally true when we think of skydiving: a novice is likely to take her first jump tightly bound to another who knows what is going to happen! Conversely, pleasures that turn solipsistic—masturbation could be the archetype—are destructive of our humanity because they cannot be shared (and therefore are increasingly unpleasurable). After my hospital experience of the pleasure of morphine, a colleague cautioned, "Watch out, Victor. That's how guys like you get addicted." Addiction is when you keep doing something even though the pleasure is all but gone.

This is the traditional teaching—that sex is good, that it belongs to marriage, and that celibacy is perfectly normal for all of us for at least part of our lives. But it is (will the reader allow me to say "alas"?) not a teaching much heard in our churches and not a teaching much lived out in our congregations. Reports come from single adults who desire opportunities to develop Christian friends but discover that the presumptive practice of their local church is that singles are looking for partners, people whom they might eventually marry. The conservative churches will expect the partners to abstain from sex until married; the liberal churches will have no such expectation; but both are united in a cultural concession and, in this, a failure to be Christianly courageous.[6] Love of our neighbor, the sincere concern for human well-being, calls us to speak clearly. The ultimate point of life for everyone and for all parts of life, given by God and made vivid in Jesus, is friendship, not marriage.

Difference, Better-ness, and Deficiency

When we say that marriage or the experience of sexual relations is not necessary to being fully human, we must not insinuate that there is something wrong or dirty about marriage. (Making sex dirty is part of the devilish work of pornography, which a Christian sexual ethic must counter.) Marriage, and thus the experience of sexual relations, is a good thing, given to us by God. And again I underline the point: the shame, the "knowledge," of nakedness that comes with the fall is not over the human body or the sexual act.

Part of my usual preparation of a couple for marriage is to work through the traditional opening speech of the celebrant in the marriage rite. In the prayer book of my church, one finds these words: "The bond and covenant of marriage was established by God in creation, and our Lord Jesus Christ adorned this manner of life by his presence and first miracle at a wedding in Cana of Galilee."[7] I point out to the couple that there are many things it is good for us to have, and yet we have them only because of the fall. Laws, for instance: we need them, but God didn't give them originally. Languages in themselves, in whose multiplicity we find the delight of diverse ways of seeing the world, seem to exist in their plurality because of the baleful divisions within humanity. By contrast, that opening speech locates marriage uniquely prior to the fall in the goodness of creation. Furthermore, if one were to say of marriage that it isn't a good thing because Jesus was not married, the rite points out that Jesus "adorned" the married state by being present and indeed by doing his first miracle at a wedding (see John 2). So while Jesus didn't marry, neither did he demean or dismiss marriage.

We see it again: something can be a good thing and yet not a necessary thing. It is good for people to be expert at brain surgery. But if you are not a brain surgeon, you are no less human. Or a different sort of analogy: it is good for human beings to have language, but one is no less human if one's language is French rather than Mandarin Chinese, or Sign rather than English. Or yet another: a child, once she exists, is a unique good, but prior to her coming into being, she was not necessary. So marriage can be good without being needful; although good, it is not a "manner of life" that all people should enter. And even though not all people need marry, that does not make it a bad thing.

With a sort of sophomoric mind (and remembering that a sophomore is, literally, a "wise moron"), I used to think in rather broad strokes that Christians early on promoted celibacy over marriage and that they made a mistake in doing so. I took the sixteenth-century Reformation as a time of correction, and Vatican II as the occasion for Roman Catholics to catch up, with the result, I thought, that we had broad ecumenical agreement today that marriage and celibacy are two equally good manners of life. I believe now that I was mistaken.

At least as a matter of clear thinking, it is not necessary, in order to affirm that two different things are each good, to go further and say that they are equally good. One good can be greater than the other, without there being anything wrong with either one. A person who is a fine chef and also an excellent surgeon, we might say, is better than someone who is a fine chef but not a surgeon (although excellence with a knife seems common to both). Or if we disagree on that, perhaps the following is easier. Money is a good thing, and human life is a good thing, but money is of less value than life (which is why murder is worse than robbery). To speak generally, there is no reason in principle to deny that some goods are better than others—however hard it might be to recognize the better-ness or to gain agreement about it in particular cases. For a beautiful example, one might meditate upon Dante's *Paradiso*, an extended study in how one saint can be greater than another without there being any sadness anywhere. Difference and gradations and variety are all part of the heavenly gyroscope.

What I'm trying to do is to open up some conceptual space so that we might see that both celibacy and marriage are good and that indeed, while many in the history of the church have held the former to be a higher good, their position might not have been as bone-headed as I once thought it was. Celibacy (whether for a time or for life, whether chosen or not, whether consecrated or not) is different from marriage. Much of Christian tradition has, in fact, asserted it to be better, a higher good. The tradition could be correct on this without thereby implying that the married state is deficient. We can uphold celibacy without demeaning marriage.

Sex and Friendship

Aristotle, we have noted, did not think it possible that a wife could be a man's friend, nor, centuries later, did the French philosopher-essayist Michel de Montaigne (1533–92). Montaigne had a very close friendship with the poet Étienne de la Boétie for an intense but short four years, ending with Boétie's death in 1563. One of Montaigne's famous essays speaks of his friendship with him and contains Montaigne's beautiful line, often quoted. Asked why they were friends, he could say only, "Because it was he; because it was I."[8] It was an intimacy founded initially on the high reputation of each. When they subsequently met for the first time, Montaigne says, "We discovered ourselves to be so seized by each other, so known to each other and so bound together that from then on none was so close as each was to the other." It was a classic, uncommon, high, exclusive friendship, such as Cicero might have extolled, and just as rare. Montaigne opines, "So many fortuitous circumstances are needed to make" such a friendship "that it is already something if Fortune can achieve it once in three centuries." (Therefore, how fortunate he was!) Along

the way of these reflections both philosophical and autobiographi-
cal, he says that "the passion men feel for women"—which, since he
takes it as a desire to seduce, is a contest of wills—cannot be compared with friendship, for when such passion "enters the territory of
friendship (where wills work together, that is) it languishes and grows
faint." Turning immediately to marriage, he finds it burdensome and
constraining—"only the entrance is free"—and yet he says that if it
were possible for a marriage to be a friendship so that "not only the
souls had this full enjoyment but in which the bodies too shared in the
union—where the whole human being was involved—it is certain that
the loving-friendship would be more full and more abundant." But
alas, Montaigne regretfully concludes, women are not capable of this.

Having found that neither an affair with a woman nor a marriage
can be a friendship, Montaigne considers "that alternative license of
the Greeks," which he says "is rightly abhorrent to our manners." But
when he goes on to describe the male-male sexual relationships of the
Greeks, he emphasizes their asymmetry: on the one hand, the Beloved,
who is young and beautiful; on the other, the Lover, who is neither
young nor beautiful and whose beauty, should he have any, will be
thus not external. Through this relationship, the Beloved learns to
see deeper than the skin, to appreciate what is within. Whatever may
have been good in this, Montaigne does not see it as friendship; it is
neither "equable" nor "equitable." He seems to be saying that there
is something not only unbalanced but also unfair in this; yet friends
must be supremely at one, holding all things in common, having a
common mind, and so forth.

Nonetheless, one should note that Montaigne does not consider,
perhaps would not have ever imagined, a sexual relationship between
two men who were equals in age and in excellence of character such
as to make a superior friendship. Although he enjoyed the pleasures of
the bed with women, his friendship with Boétie was quite a different
matter. Montaigne separated sex from friendship, while regretting
that marriage could not be a friendship. He had no other friend; after
Boétie's death, "I merely drag wearily on. . . . There is no deed nor
thought in which I do not miss him."

Christianity, from the early centuries, had a different view: marriage was a particular variety of friendship. Oliver O'Donovan claims

that early Christians simply took it for granted that "marriage was a field of friendship between husband and wife." This is a signal Christian innovation. For these Christians, "the highest value of marriage," the most important thing about it, or that for which it was most highly esteemed, was that it was a friendship.[9] Carol Harrison similarly summarizes Augustine's view in his treatise of AD 401, "On the Good of Marriage": "In respect of each of these goods [of marriage] in this treatise [namely, progeny, fidelity, and the sacrament] marriage is above all treated as a relationship which is founded upon, informed by and which finds its ideal realisation in the friendship of the partners."[10] As the Christian assumption (that marriage aims at being friendship) played out in history, it tended to elevate the estimation with which marriage was held—and in parallel with marriage, the estimation of married women themselves (despite such retrograde sentiments as expressed by Montaigne).

Although it sees marriage as a species of friendship, this innovative Christian logic will not allow marriage to be taken as the *highest* form of friendship—precisely because of the Christian conviction that the friendship that marks a fulfilled human being cannot be exclusive. On the contrary, as we have seen in many places already, it aims decidedly at ever greater expansion. Our Lord's disciples, in the end, were his friends, and thus friends of one another, and as such the forerunners of the friendship that is universal in his kingdom. Marriage, by contrast, is committed to a lifelong exclusivity, an intimacy that is closed to others.

To unpack these thoughts further, we need first to expose more of the logic of Christian opposition to unmarried sex. That logic is captured by the Christian use of a Greek word, *porneia*.

The Christian Invention of Fornication

In our post-Freudian age, one can still hear the indictment that Christianity is sexually repressive. Christians are accused of being against sex, and on that account (it is said in various ways), they oppose abortion, women's equality, divorce, public eroticism, fertility rites, and on down the line. In their anti-sexuality (the indictment continues), Christians themselves are sexually repressed, and one consequence of this is the sexual acting-out of supposedly celibate priests (but, to be honest, Protestant clergy are hardly innocent in this) and the cover-up scandals that seem to have been motivated by a desire to protect the church's reputation and its repressive teaching—cover-ups carried out by men who did not really believe said teaching but felt the need to pretend they did. Much better, the indictment goes, is to acknowledge that we are sexual beings, that sexual expression is liberative and at the heart of our self-creation (which is how we become ourselves, by choosing our values and making our own path in life), and that the best policy is to throw off all external authority, to "let it all hang out."

Entangled with this narrative of Christian repressiveness is a myth about classical society. The story is that the Roman and Greek societies of the ancient world were blissful, guilt-free, and sexually open worlds in which public eroticism and numerous sexual variations were happily celebrated. Then came the tragic takeover of the legal system by Christians, who proceeded to introduce and then enforce repressive legal structures. The world then fell into a darkness of repression and ill-health until our twentieth-century liberation, thanks to Freud and/or the Pill and/or the Supreme Court.

That is a myth, and like most myths, there is truth in it: the Christian transformation of the Roman legal system was aimed at sexual control—at reshaping the sexual practices of society. But the antecedent classical world was hardly a libertine free-for-all. In fact, the ancients had their own highly developed, well-defined practices for the social control of sex, practices that aimed at cultivating a particular notion of shame.

Let us sketch some of the complexities of ancient shame and sexual practices. A Roman girl became marriageable at the age of twelve, as we know from Augustine, who shortly after he turned thirty was engaged to a girl who was not yet of age; she was ten. Augustine, having dismissed his concubine of the past decade and more, could not wait and thus took on another woman (as he tells in *Confessions* VI.xv.25).[11]

Boys did not marry until they were much older—typically in their late twenties. But it was considered unhealthy to dam up the sexual fluids and fail to express one's sexuality. The well-born girl was to pass directly from virginity to the hallowed status of wife; the alternative was shame. What then were the necessary sexual outlets for the males, both before and within marriage? They were the public brothels, prostitutes, male slaves of the household, and boys who were not freeborn and who were in that indeterminate period between childhood and manhood. Same-sex relations per se were not despised, yet it was shameful to be penetrated by another male.

What was wrong with a male being penetrated or a female having sex before she was married was that it was shameful. Shame, however, was a class-differentiated concept. Lower-class people were incapable of suffering shame, and so slaves, male and female, could be used to sate male desire.

In his study of the change Christianity made to sexual morality, the classicist Kyle Harper puts it in the contrast of two words: shame and sin.[12] In the popular romances, he shows, the Roman dramatic arc concerned the passage of a woman from childhood to the secure status of wife, a perilous passage that, if successfully navigated, avoided shame. By the end of the sixth century, Christian romances had replaced this with a new dramatic arc of the repentance of sexual sinners, whose conversion to a new life marked, implicitly, the triumph of freedom over fate. Shame, once acquired, adhered to the person forever, but sin could be taken away.

My description in the preceding few paragraphs is exceedingly simplified; it is but an attempt to point to a real transformation achieved by Christianity. Faced with a society that saw sexual release as normal and necessary, that stratified people, that subsisted on the ready supply of a vast number of slaves (perhaps 20 percent of the population of Roman cities), Christians, who understood themselves as citizens of a kingdom where distinctions of slave and free, male and female, young and old made no difference, were able to say, "We can live without this. We can say no."

They were, in the end, not much interested in the distinction between high-born boys and other boys, between high-born women and other women, between being passive or active in a male-male sexual act, for they had a new concept, drawn from the writings of Saint Paul, that all sexual relations whatsoever, outside the marriage of a man and a woman, could be grouped together and put under a single word, *fornication* (*porneia* in Greek, *fornicatio* in Latin). This "churchly" word was used in a novel sense by Christians for a concept that the ancients simply did not have: an undifferentiated grouping together of all sexual relations outside of marriage—grouped together and cast aside.[13]

The Limited but Real Value of Rules

You can't play a game if there aren't rules. Rules are boundary conditions that set out what counts as playing the game. If I pick up a soccer ball with my hands (which, dear reader, you may call a football if you wish) and run with it as far as I can, you should stop me and tell me that I'm not playing soccer. If I want to play soccer, I have to follow the rules, which include not touching the ball with my hands. At the same time, I could keep all the rules and still not be playing soccer. You just need to imagine me standing still in the middle of the field, paying no attention to the ball, avoiding touching it, and so forth. You should say to me, "Victor, you may be keeping all the rules, but you still aren't playing soccer."

So here's a rule for, if I may so put it, "playing the human game": if you want to live a fully human life, you must separate sex from friendship (outside the special, term-limited case of marriage). Try to bring sex into friendship, and it becomes a pseudo-marriage. It then loses the expansiveness that belongs to friendship: the desire to have ever more friends. Sex, apart from its casual use (as when someone says, "What's the problem? It's just friction"), is a movement toward one other person to the exclusion of others. Friendship is a movement toward another person that does not exclude others. To put it another way, "friends with benefits" aren't really friends (as indeed they aren't really in the film by that name).

We will help people if we spell out this rule, and by doing so, we can build up one another through the creation of common expectations for friendships. Yet following this rule would not mean that you were succeeding in making friends. Like Victor stuck in the middle of the soccer field, determinedly not touching the ball with his hands but doing nothing else, you could keep this rule—you could completely shun fornication throughout your life—but still fail to grow in friendship.

Celibacy (understood in its bare sense of avoiding sexual relations) is a very different thing than friendship; it merely marks out the field within which friendship can grow (and remembering that there is a piece of the field reserved for marriage and its own disciplines of fidelity). Rules are important, but they are never enough.

Maturing into Friendship

Some decades ago, I was asking a priest-professor how he understood gay relationships, what he thought about homosexuality. He said that in his observation, over time a same-sex relationship tends to develop into a chaste friendship. The sex, he said, turns out to be not that important.

Many fathers of the church saw the same development as to be desired for married couples. After they had children (if God gave them children), and then only by mutual consent, they might grow into a state of mutual celibacy. If they no longer had obligations to their children, they could enter monastic establishments, but they could equally (at least it seemed to some) go on living in a home with each other, but continently.

As I indicated above, for years I resisted this view (with its implicitly higher valuation of celibacy over marriage), but if one studies the literature, it is clearly present. Yet there may be more. It seems to me marriage developing into celibacy could be (at least for some people) in deep accord with the Christian claim that marriage is only "till death us do part." Death concludes a marriage—but the friendship (which the marriage was a type of) continues, one prays, into the life to come, where it will not be exclusive but rather a part of the expansiveness of Jesus' friends. At least in some cases, some church fathers seem to have thought that this continuing quality of friendship could be experienced in an anticipatory way if the bodily cleaving were to become less of an ongoing feature of the marital friendship even in this life.

This seems to be Augustine's mature view, as Harrison summarizes it:

> The sexual aspect of marriage was by no means definitive of it for Augustine. . . . He maintains that there is an enduring "quiddam

coniugale," an enduring marital "thing." . . . There is, as he puts
it, a "natural society (*societas*) itself in a difference of sex" which
is independent of procreation, or the age of the partners. . . . He
develops these views most especially in relation to Mary and Joseph, who were married even though there was no sexual relation
between the partners. They are called husband and wife because,
as he puts it, "intercourse of the mind is more intimate than that
of the body."[14]

That Augustinian term "intercourse of the mind" points to the friendship that is always there in a marriage yet into which a marriage can
more deeply mature. A universal human friendship is Augustine's
ultimate dream, as we see at the end of his *City of God*. It is a state
of unimaginable intimacy in which "the thoughts of each of us will
then also be made manifest to all."[15]

   With hope for that ultimate intimacy, here are some rules for human
beings in this life.

> *Sexual relations outside marriage are wrong, without regard to
> class, gender, or other human differentiation.*
> *Human happiness and flourishing is thoroughly compatible with
> sexual abstinence.*
> *The flourishing of human beings does not lie in marriage but in
> being able to live with others as friends, and marriage itself
> should be understood, in its ultimate sense, as being oriented
> to friendship.*

   These rules have the limitations of all rules. Here the purpose
is to identify boundary conditions of human friendship. I set them
forth with the hope that they will provide the framework needed
for a culture of friendship to grow, but of course they cannot themselves grow that culture. We Christians need to uphold one another
with encouragement to develop spiritual friendships—which is to
say, nonmarital friendships—and to avoid undermining them with
the suspicion of sexual intimacy. We need to learn from one another
how to be friends who are intimate and chaste and how to encourage
more of such friendship. In other words, we need to be secure in the

boundary conditions so that friendship can grow and flourish as the highest and greatest activity of human beings.

And that means we need unapologetically to champion celibacy as a positive gift for everyone in all parts of life save those times of marriage—and to recognize marriage itself as ordered toward celibate, postmarital friendship.

NINE

Is There Friendship in the Trinity?

Is God Friendship?

How far does friendship go? Through the entire universe does it run, according to the beautiful claim of Aelred at the end of the first book of his *Spiritual Friendship*. God's wish—the perspective is so vast it is worth quoting again—is that "all his creatures . . . be joined together in peace, and for community to exist between them." Aelred claims that "even among insensible things" like the earth or rivers or stones "a certain love of community, as it were, shines forth"; they have a "community" (*societas*) in that none of them exists alone; beings— things—that lack senses nonetheless enjoy some sort of analogue to friendship. Thus more so nonhuman sentient beings, although lacking human rationality, "in this one respect" still "imitate the human spirit, in that they . . . follow each other, they play with each other, in their movements and noises they express and give evidence of their mutual affection." Indeed, he continues, "so avidly and happily [do they] enjoy their common community, that they appear to care for nothing more than those things we associate with friendship." And friendship extends further, beyond the material creation to the spiritual, where "divine wisdom saw to it that not just one [angel], but many were created, among whom community was welcome and the sweetest love created a unity of will and affection." Thus friendship characterizes the universe even in the spiritual realm, where "sheer numbers banished solitude, and mutual participation in joy increased the happiness of the many" (I.53–57).

We noted earlier (in chap. 7) Aelred's teaching that human beings in their original nature were made for friendship with each other. The fall, however, fractured this primordial universal bond, as "avarice and envy corrupted the splendor of friendship and affection" and brought the ills of "disputes, rivalries, hatred, and suspicion." The result was the need to distinguish between affection and friendship, to show universal affection or grace (or we might say Christian love) even to enemies, while friendship adapted itself to a more constrained circumference. Nonetheless—to repeat in order not to lose sight of the conclusion—the desire that friendship extend to embrace more and more people has never left the Christian heart (I.58–59).

Friendship, in these different concrete ways, marks the entire creation, from mere matter to pure spirit and including (still—despite the fall) human beings. This sweeping conclusion is itself astonishing, but does it capture the whole truth? Or does friendship extend even further? Is friendship something we might attribute properly to God himself, in his own, uncreated, eternal being?

This question is posed by Aelred's interlocutor, Ivo, with emotional and indeed existential urgency. "But what does all this mean?" he asks. "Shall I say of friendship what Jesus' friend, the apostle John said of grace [caritas], that 'God is friendship'?" (I.69). The line from 1 John 4:16 is eminently famous: "God is love." Ivo wants to know if we should say also, "God is friendship."

Aelred replies that to do so would be "unusual" and that the sentence lacks "scriptural authority." Nonetheless, he reckons that it must be true, for everything that comes out of grace or love (caritas) can be called friendship. His example is 1 John 4:16 itself, where the complete sentence reads, "God is love; and he that dwelleth in love dwelleth in God, and God in him." Aelred says, replacing love/grace (caritas) with friendship (amicitia), that a person who dwells in friendship truly enjoys with God a mutual indwelling (I.70). It makes sense to say that a person who abides in friendship is abiding in God and God is abiding in him. So, yes, we may say that God is friendship.

Are the Persons of the Trinity Friends?

Good and proper catechetical teaching puts forth that "God is love" is literally true thanks to God being himself the Trinity. That is to say, "God is love" asserts more than that God is loving; it asserts more than that he loves the things in the world and indeed more than that he loves even thee and me. "God is love" means that God is constituted by love, that his very being is love. So we can say that the Father loves the Son (he bestows himself upon the Son); the Son receives that love and returns it to the Father through a perfect counter-bestowal; and the love that flows between them in this pattern of bestowal and counter-bestowal is the Holy Spirit.

In speaking that way, we are putting in rather simple terms the teaching of great theologians, who were themselves trying to hold together everything that the Scriptures declare concerning God's being. For our purposes, I will home in on one paragraph of just one of the classical works—namely, Augustine's *On the Trinity*.[1] In book VI, Augustine first sets out the unity and equality of the Father and the Son and then turns, in chapter 5 of that book, to the Holy Spirit. His first claim is that the Holy Spirit has the same unity of substance and the same equality as the Father and the Son. There are different suggestions, all drawing from the scriptural witness, concerning how we might understand the Spirit. He might be the unity of the Father and the Son, or their holiness, or their love; or he might be one of these most fundamentally and then consequentially the other two (for instance, he might fundamentally be the holiness of the Father and the Son, and therefore the love that they have, and therefore their unity). But however we take him, it is clear that the Holy Spirit is neither the Father nor the Son. This is because he is the one through whom the other two are joined; it is through the Spirit that the Father begets (and loves) the Son, and through the same Spirit that the Son loves the Father, who begets him.

At this point, Augustine quotes Saint Paul's line "to keep the unity of the Spirit in the bond of peace" (Eph. 4:3). This line culminates the apostle's admonition to the church in Ephesus to "walk" in a manner "worthy of the vocation wherewith ye are called," for the sake of keeping "the unity of the Spirit in the bond of peace" (4:1–3).

The reality behind this admonition, Augustine says, is in the being of the Trinity. The persons of the Trinity are not equal by the gift of someone higher than themselves; it is their own gift to each other that makes them equal, and all that they have to give is their own essence, which is one and the same in each.

The Holy Spirit, that is to say, is common to both the Father and the Son; it cannot be that one would have him and the other not. The three are "God, one, alone, great, wise, holy, blessed." Then Augustine mentions friendship. "But that communion itself"—the communion enjoyed by the persons of the Trinity, which is identical with the persons of the Trinity—"is consubstantial and co-eternal; and if it may fitly be called friendship, let it be so called." Augustine goes on at once to say he prefers to call it "love," doubtless because that is the biblical word (1 John 4:16, as we saw just above).[2] Then to wrap up the doctrine, he states that the Holy Spirit, being love (as are the Father and the Son), is along with them also substance, great, good, holy. Whatever else we might say God is, we will say that equally of Father, Son, and Holy Spirit.

There are not more than three, Augustine says, because these words *substance*, *great*, *good*, and so forth do not speak of something that God takes on. The Father never has an existence "prior" to the Son, so he is eternally love, and so forth.

What the reader should notice is that since God is love, we may say *God is friendship*. It then would not be a sufficient regard for friendship to elevate it *only* to the status of a great cosmic *principle*, applicable to all things material and spiritual and especially to human beings at their highest. No, friendship is also *a name*—one might think possibly the best name of all—for the mystery at the heart of God's being. When Jesus reveals at the Last Supper that the point of his incarnation is to make human friendship possible (thereby interpreting his death on the cross as the highest form of love, the giving of his life for his friends), that friendship is given its location. The mansion where human friendship dwells is the being of God, to whom, Augustine emphasizes, we may (and must) cleave by grace. "We ourselves are one"—in unity with each other, in friendship—"by [God's] gift, and one spirit with Him, because our soul cleaves to Him so as to follow Him." The love that God gives us (which is to say, the friendship that God gives) is with him and with one another.

The analogical leaps here are breathtaking, although given the reality of the Spirit, perhaps we should say "breath-giving"! Augustine has it all in place so that, in a sense, Aelred and then Aquinas only had to move forward one tiny step to declare that love or grace, *caritas*, just is friendship, *amicitia*.

Is There a Difference between Being God's Friend and Being His Child?

If God is friendship in his very being, then the persons of the Trinity are friends with each other, and so it would be proper to say the Father and the Son are friends. And if the disciples of Jesus are friends with one another and with Jesus, then it seems they must be friends also with the Father, on the principle that the friend of my friend is someone I also want to be friends with. It is a general theological truth that with regard to all matters outside God's being, what is true of one of the divine persons is true of each of them. If you are Jesus' friend, then you are also a friend of the Holy Spirit and a friend of the Father.

But sometimes we must distinguish the persons of the Trinity. Consider this line of thought: Since Jesus is God, whatever is true of Jesus is true of God. If Jesus drinks a cup of water, it is true to say "God drinks a cup of water." But it would not be true to say "The Father drinks a cup of water." Why? Because the Father has not taken on himself a human nature as the Son has. It is by reason of his human nature, and not his divine nature, that Jesus can drink water. The Father, having no human nature, cannot drink water—or anything else.

That is to say, the things Jesus does by virtue of his humanity, although they are things that God does (since Jesus is truly God), are not things that we can say the Father or the Spirit does. So it seems we need to ask our question in a new way. Does Jesus make himself our friend by virtue of his human nature or his divine nature? For if it is only by virtue of his humanity that Jesus makes himself our friend, then we would not be able to say that we share in the friendship that is the heart of the Trinity.

Now the friendship that Jesus offers is the fulfillment of the created goodness of humanity. When God stated it was not good for the original human to be alone, God was stating that human flourishing is found in friendship. Jesus makes that possible by being a complete, sinless human being. There is no separation in him between himself and God, and nothing dividing him off from other people, and nothing creating internal divisions within himself. He is "at-one," and his offer of atonement ("at-one-ment") is an offer of friendship.

Thus it seems to me that it is by virtue both of his divinity and of his humanity that Jesus makes himself our friend. By his humanity, he was able to die for his friends and thereby offer the love than which there is no greater. But the substance of his friendship with his disciples included his sharing with them everything he received from the Father—in other words, his sharing of that which he had by virtue of his divinity.

It is worth noting that the conclusion is different, in terms of the words we use, when we turn to familial language of sisters and brothers, daughters and sons. When we think of ourselves as Jesus' brothers and sisters, we at the same time think of ourselves as children of the Father. But note that we use different language depending on which person of the Trinity we are considering: for the Son, a sibling, but for the Father, a child. Yet the end point is the same—namely, finding our lives in the midst of God's being. We are lifted by God's action (his grace, his love) to a level that is equal to God so that he can love us and we can love him. At that place of equality, we are friends of God *and* children of God *and* siblings of God—all those different words for the same reality. Saint Paul writes of this reality when he speaks of the mystery of prayer in his Epistle to the Romans: "We know not what we should pray for . . . but the Spirit itself maketh intercession for us with groanings which cannot be uttered" (8:26). Prayer is our being placed within the being of God: the Spirit, within us, prays through Jesus to the Father. That is to say, prayer is the life of divine communication and our being placed, quite beyond our capacity to comprehend it, in the midst of that communication. It is our being lifted up to the level of friend of God.

One final point is necessary. If we are children of God, we are not so in any childish or inferior way. The point of grace is that we are no longer mere creatures, mere subordinates or servants or slaves. We are also no longer children in the sense of being immature (we are no longer under guardians, as Lysis and Menexenus were). We remain creatures, yes; we remain God's servants, one might even say his slaves, but Jesus no longer calls us servants! We remain creatures, yet we know the intimacy that comes from the Son sharing his mind with us. Our obedience is free. We have the dignity of being a friend of our truest friend.

TEN

Examples of Friendship

Friendship as Moral Development

The initiation of a friendship may be a mystery. Someone comes into your life, and you are attracted to him, to how he sees the world, or perhaps to how he is, how he comports himself, how he acts in the world. A classmate, an office worker, a barista, someone who goes to your church: it can happen in any part of life, the recognition that here is a person you'd like to get to know better. This person and I might be able to become friends.

The development of a friendship is different. Development doesn't "just happen"; you must choose to spend time together doing various things and talking. David texts you to ask if you'd like to meet for lunch. There's a "Millennial" place called Made Nice that he'd like to introduce you to: good food, cool vibe, you can pick up lunch and walk to the park and eat and talk. It's a fall day, not too hot. You text back, "Sounds great. Some of my best friends are Millennials." David, who is a Gen Xer, likes the joke (he is gay; he knows lots of people who say, "Some of my best friends are gay"), and he writes back, "Yes. It's hard but I'm glad you've put in the effort."

Friendship takes time and a certain measure of deliberation. One seeks opportunities to meet face to face; between meetings, one tries to talk, or write, or email, or text. The physical meeting needs to happen: from the ancients to today, those who think about friendship realize the irreplaceability of being in the same space, breathing the same atmosphere. And then beyond simply meeting, one seeks opportunities to do things together. David likes Made Nice, and he wants you to share it together. After lunch, you mention a gallery exhibition that seems interesting; you want to see it, but it is better to walk there and see it with a friend. Along the way, a church is open, an Orthodox church in a neighborhood you used to live in. You pause to admire its external mosaic icons, then say—a mutual yet spontaneous decision made by each of you at the same time, but a decision you might not have made had you been alone—"Let's see if we can go inside." It turns out you can't, but that leads to more conversation.

This is an ordinary sort of thing, a quotidian example of what Aristotle called the pleasantest human thing: friends, lunch, a destination, conversation on the walk, a spontaneous detour. Ordinary, yet morally freighted. Think of some of the decisions involved here. One decides to be with a friend rather than have the default of inertia take over; one reaches out. One decides to try what the friend finds interesting: food, a walk, art. That is to say, one desires to see the world from the point of view of the friend and to be in the world and act in the world with the friend. And for a Christian, may I say the opportunity posed by an unknown church is symbolically deep? God invites us to have him as part of our friendship, even as he invites us to be friends with him. The activity of friendship changes us.

I have heard of an old *Punch* magazine joke: There are two people, and one of them says, "Well, that's enough of me talking about me.... What do you think about me?" It's funny, but it hurts, reminding us of the great human problem of egoism. It is hard to turn outside of ourselves, to turn our minds to other people and to their loves and concerns. Yet if we fail to do that, we fail at our humanity. Moral development culminates in the ability to live with others as friends. Aristotle is right to make friendship the aim and end of ethics. And Jesus shows us how profoundly true it is while at the same time making it possible: the end of being human is to be friends.

Is Friendship Lost in Translation?

Moral education requires examples. To grow in these matters, it helps to have illustrations in which we can see friendship being achieved partially, struggled for, attained, or lost. I begin with Bob and Charlotte.

They are brought together in Sofia Coppola's 2003 film *Lost in Translation*: a fifty-five-year-old actor in a midlife slump, Bob Harris (played masterfully by Bill Murray), and a just-out-of-Yale philosophy major, Charlotte (played with equal mastery by Scarlett Johansson). Both their marriages are unsatisfactory; Bob's wife has not traveled with him, and we quickly see that Charlotte's husband of two years already has little interest in her. Bob and Charlotte are staying in the same Tokyo hotel for no more than a week. They meet in a bar, strike up a bit of conversation, start venturing into the city's nightlife together. They are being drawn together.

One wonders, *Will this intimacy culminate in sex? And if not, how will they fall apart?* For when one sees this plotline in a film, one expects that it will lead to sex (whether or not they leave their spouses to continue together as a new couple) or that something will come along to separate them before there is sexual consummation.

What makes this film's plot extraordinary is that neither of those two things happens. They do not have sex, and they do not distance themselves from each other. Over the days that they are together in the same hotel in the same city, they manifestly awaken to longings for each other (Coppola's film has been praised as a study in longing). The film allows us to wonder: Is it precisely because they do not have sex that they grow in intimacy with each other?

In one confiding moment, we see them reaching across the gap that lies between them. It is not that he is famous and rich, even if he has fallen into that so-called shameful stage of making commercial endorsements for cash; it is that he has been married for twenty-five years and she only for two. He has children at home (apparently born some considerable time into his marriage); she has none. She asks if marriage gets easier. That's hard, he says. It used to be a lot of fun; his wife would come with him to movie shoots, and they laughed a lot together. Now she prefers to stay home with the kids. He describes with tones of disaster what happens when a child enters a marriage.

The day the first child is born, he says, is the most terrifying day of your life. "Your life, as you know it, is gone, never to return." This solemn truth, with its implications of the eclipse of love and the end of being the object of the passion of one's spouse, settles gloomily into their silence. Then he starts to talk again. He says that those children learn to talk and walk, and they become amazing people, people who are full of delight.

They have this conversation as they are lying in bed, on top of a white fluffy bedcover, lying on their backs, clothed. She turns on her side toward him while keeping a distance. Her knees are close to his side, her bare toes touching the side of his hip. There is silence. He moves his hand down and lets it rest on her foot. His head remains tilted away from her. More silence, then his barely whispered line, "You aren't hopeless."[1]

In Coppola's directorial hands, Bob and Charlotte seem to point to something about real friendship. It is crucial that they do not leave their respective spouses, crucial that they avoid adultery, crucial indeed that they see that a sexual union would actually cheapen their intimacy and harm their lives. They keep a physical distance. They long. But they are not at all in situations that are without hope.

Might this be a grappling toward friendship? It strikes me that friendship is the ghost in the film that wants to come out and name its place on the stage! That we so deeply long not for another sexual pairing-up in a world of all sorts of already messy pairings-up but for intimacy in the midst of the messy world, an alternative intimacy that brings hope—all this feels true. Neither Bob nor Charlotte is beyond hope. Of course, their friendship, if that's what it is, would be nearly impossible to continue past their few days in Tokyo. And there being a void of cultural patterns for them to follow, one doubts that it will. So at best the film gives us a fleeting picture of friendship, an evocation of our greater hope. Furthermore, this fleeting picture comes in a film framed without reference to Christianity, and thus without Christianity's resources to ground and shape hope and bring it forth to its end. (O sad elite culture, which sees not the jewel-stones within that rejected faith!) But to imagine a world in which men and women (and men and men, and women and women) can be intimate without having sex, who through their closeness help each other to see the world more honestly and enjoy afresh the lives they actually have, that is to imagine a world that understands a place for friendship. It seems to me that *Lost in Translation* is just such an exercise in friendly imagination.

Harry Potter and the School of Friendship

In a talk I had with a young-adults group while preparing this book, a thirty-ish, sharp, very professional-looking woman spoke almost wistfully about the desirability of disentangling sex and friendship, of being able to have friends without the imposed expectation (imposed by others, by the other, or by oneself) that intimacy will inevitably turn sexual. One has heard of the third-date rule: by the third date, the couple will decide to have sex or to break up. Three dates might be six or twelve hours together, far short of the time it takes to establish a real friendship. I heard in her a questioning, whether the sexualization of our social world has short-circuited our ability to grow in friendship. Can we find a place for a nonsexual intimacy?

This young woman said she was finding it harder to make friends in her thirties, and others around her agreed. Friendships were easier in school, she said. And that's when she brought up Harry Potter. The Potter books are, of course, not really about magic. They are about being human and finding identity across difference and growing into maturity; about struggling to be good and struggling against evil; about love and family and self-sacrifice. And one major theme throughout is friendship. In connection with friendship, this young woman brought up Luna Lovegood and a scene that she recalled from one of the movies. Harry has isolated himself from both teachers and students. He is feeling not only the normal teenage angst of dealing with study, sport, girls, and so on but also the peculiar burden of being disbelieved and mocked on all sides. On top of this, he has the burden of knowing that the Dark Lord has returned, a knowledge that drives him into isolation. On a solitary walk in the forest, he comes across the significantly named Luna Lovegood. There is no romance between them; she is an odd girl with strange intuitions and an other-worldly sense about her. But what she does is speak directly to him as would a friend. Although yet children, both have already seen death. Both can see the "thestrals," flying reptilian horses that are invisible to most people. Luna crosses the distance between herself and Harry as if it were no distance at all, and she tells him she believes him. She then tells him plainly that he should not isolate himself: his being cut off and alone is just what the Dark Lord would want. Luna makes Harry see that his friends, even though they misunderstand him, need him, and that in turn he himself needs to be with them. She thereby points him to one of the basic lessons of friendship: we need to see things as others see them; we need to get into our friends' minds, to realize that we are profoundly connected with our friends.

The world of Harry Potter, unlike that of *Lost in Translation*, is a world with Christian artifacts. The holidays are Christmas and Easter. The orphan has a godfather. And it is a world that rejects cheap grace, such as the sentimentality that dead people stay on with us as spirits. (One who does linger, Nearly-Headless Nick, tells Harry that he floats through the Hogwarts school because he made the bad choice not to die and go on but to die and stay around.) With neither cheap grace nor sentimentality, the world of Harry Potter understands the deep truth that there are worse things than death—and stronger things than death—and the hard truth that to be a friend, one might have to die.

If we think of Luna again, we can see further depths in what she was doing. The danger to Harry, unknown to him at that point, was that Voldemort, the Dark Lord, was able to get into his mind. But Harry's protection in the book's climactic battle will be that, once there, Voldemort cannot stand to be intimate with him—to be in his mind. As Dumbledore, the headmaster, will tell him at the end, there is an always-locked room in "the Department of Mysteries" that "contains a force that is at once more wonderful and more terrible than death." That power, he tells Harry, "you possess in such quantities" yet "Voldemort has [it] not at all." It saved Harry from possession by Voldemort "because he could not bear to reside in a body so full of the force he detests."[2] So the irony—and it is implicit in Luna's speaking to Harry—is that it is not necessarily bad to have someone enter your mind. Good people who have a common mind (or perhaps better put, who know and share each other's mind) have in one another a very intimate friend.

It would stretch the point to claim that the Harry Potter books are Christian or that they are of lasting literary merit (although I confess I had underestimated them on that score). Yet they are, for our moment, valuable cultural resources for those who would grow in friendship. They work even accidentally. There is a sushi place near my home I like to frequent; when I go there alone, I take a book to read. Recently, as he led me to my table, the young man asked me if I had a book with me. Yes, I said, it's in my backpack. He asked what I was reading. "Actually," I said, "it's Harry Potter." Suddenly, he was all animation. He wanted to know which one it was, and he told me which ones he thought were the best, and so on. He and I were friendly in a new way because I just happened to be reading one of these books. They go deep into our culture, and it is a good thing they do.

Friendship and the Struggle for Good in *The Lord of the Rings*

The books of J. R. R. Tolkien seem less well-known today than when I was younger (at least among the young adults I talk to), but still one can find circles that are sufficiently cerebral to get into them. One such circle was that same young-adults group. When I asked them about friendship and *The Lord of the Rings*, the excitement was instantaneous. "Gandalf!" a young man exclaimed. "Let me ask you, does Gandalf have any friends?" We pondered the matter. It would be hard to claim that Bilbo or Frodo or any of the other hobbits are his friends; the differences between them are too great. Gandalf has wisdom, has lived much longer than any dwarf or hobbit, has converse with other wizards and great men and elves. Perhaps Elrond and Aragorn may be considered his friends; with them he can share his mind. Were Saruman not a traitor, he too could have been a friend. Yet by the end, I think it comes to be that the hobbit Frodo achieves friendship with Gandalf. Through his participation in the entire quest and particularly in the destruction of the ring, through his bearing the weighty consequences of that journey and climactic struggle, Frodo somehow rises from being

Gandalf's student and collaborator and fellow pipe smoker to being his equal, to being of one mind with him. They depart for the Grey Havens together.

Tolkien shows us other friendships in this trilogy. The four hobbits of the ring-fellowship are friends, with Sam and Frodo being particularly close and Merry and Pippin also bound together by temperament and life. The dwarf Gimli and the elf Legolas begin with mutual suspicion but become friends, giving everyone who sees them an unexpected picture of (how shall we put it?) trans-species or trans-racial friendship, a picture remarkable for all the prejudices it overturns. Think of how Gimli looks forward to showing Legolas the marvels of the dwarves' caves—and Legolas looks forward to visiting them with him! And conversely, the beauties of the elven woods!

All these friendships are forged for enjoyment in everyday life, but importantly, they are made in the crucible of the great struggle of good and evil. The friendships in Tolkien's world, a world of marvelous diversity in its forms of good, are friendships based on the common cause of fighting for the good (as, in their own way, are the friendships of Harry Potter). At the same time, in the final chapters (which, facing difficult truths, were omitted from the film version), we see that even everyday life contains significant and necessary struggles on behalf of the good. Yes, the ring has been destroyed, and, yes, the great victory has been won. Nonetheless, there remain people who carry out small-level wickedness that in its own way is just as bad. The hobbits return to their beloved Shire to find that they must fight even there against injustice and cruelty.

This might be the most important lesson of Tolkien's great saga. There is never a time when friendships are about nothing but companionship and sharing. When we think with Aristotle of friendship as the pleasantest thing for human beings, we should not think of that in abstraction from concrete commitments: to be good, to have pure motives, to welcome and foster beauty in the world, and, when necessary, to oppose evil forthrightly. Right after the ring is destroyed, and even as the world around them is melting away in something like flowing lava, sensing he is at the end of the world, Frodo takes Sam's hand and is glad they are there together.

Learning Friendship on the River

Mark Twain draws us into friendship as a process of character development in his great book, *The Adventures of Huckleberry Finn*. Set in and alongside a pre–Civil War Mississippi River, this novel builds up an unexpectedly deep friendship between a boy, Huckleberry, and an enslaved man, Jim. Their friendship is unexpected because friendship requires a fundamental equality, but Huck and Jim are separated by great difference in age and status. Yet it should be noted that the superiority of the man to the boy is in some way counterbalanced by the subservience of the slave to the free. These crosscurrents of inequality, experienced as the Mississippi itself draws them into the ambiguous waters that lap onto free and slave states alike, help open up for them a space in which they can be friendly, and more than friendly. Gradually, ensuing events on this wide and long river lead to Huck's recognition of Jim as his equal, and as equal, his true friend.

The moral power of Twain is to show this development with humor and without preaching. We see Jim endanger himself for the sake of Huck, which the reader may well recognize as the willingness to lay down his life for his friend. And we see Huck, quite literally, decide to lay down his eternal life for Jim. Twain makes Huck the voice of the typical mentality of white slave masters. Huck knows that escaped slaves ought to be turned in to the authorities, and therefore he recognizes that what he is doing, when he assists Jim's escape toward freedom, is a sin and will send him to hell. But Huck also senses that he cannot turn in Jim, who has done so much for him as a friend.

He ponders turning in Jim to the extent that he actually writes out the words "Miss Watson your runaway n— Jim is down here two mile below Pikesville and Mr. Phelps has got him and he will give him up for the reward if you send." But he looks at the paper and thinks about his trip down the river. "I see Jim before me, all the time, in the day, and in the night-time, sometimes moonlight, sometimes storms, and we a floating along, talking, and singing, and laughing." He can't find any memories that would turn his heart hard against Jim. To the contrary, "I'd see him standing my watch on top of his'n, stead of calling me, so I could go on sleeping; and see him how glad he was when I come back out of the fog; and when I come to him again in the swamp, up there where the feud was; and such-like times; and would always call me honey, and pet me, and do everything he could think of for me, and how good he always was; and at last I struck the time I saved him by telling the men we had small-pox aboard, and he was so grateful, and said I was the best friend old Jim ever had in the world, and the *only* one he's got now." Huck looks again at the paper and tears it up. "All right, then," he says to himself; he won't turn in Jim. In fact, he will work to get him free, even though it means the loss of his soul![3]

So Twain takes the Christian truth that the greatest love is to lay down your life for your friend and shows us, in Huck's confused theology, that Huck decides to lay down his *eternal* life for the sake of his friend. Huck has come to see that Jim is every bit as much a human being as he is and thus of equal dignity to himself—a lesson that he has learned in the school of friendship. The point is plain: Huck is willing to lay down his life—to go to hell—for the sake of Jim, who had said of Huck that he was the only friend he had.

The story remains complicated—there is the famously difficult game that Huck plays at Jim's expense in the final part of the book. Twain is no sentimentalist. Huck continues to extemporize lies, or stories, to get along in the white world. When in chapter 32 he gets to the house of Aunt Sally, she takes him to be her nephew, and he plays along with her misperception, inventing, to explain his unannounced arrival, a story that he was riding on a boat whose cylinder head had suddenly blown out. "Good gracious," says Aunt Sally, "anybody hurt?" Not missing a beat, Huck says, "No'm. Killed a n—." And she: "Well, it's lucky; because sometimes people do get hurt."[4]

But the reader knows that Huck knows full well that black slaves are just as much "people" as this Aunt Sally; it is what he has learned in the school of friendship amid the crosscurrents of a multitude of human sins along the river. In the messy particularities of antebellum American slavery, *The Adventures of Huckleberry Finn* instances for us that humans are most true to their nature when they can live with others as friends.

Pushing the Boundaries of Friendship

Genesis 2 gives an account of why we long for friendship with animals—namely, that each one of them (the land animals and birds) was created as a potential help-meet for the original human. Two points are worth pondering. First, the fact that none of the animals was fitting means that none of them was found capable of full friendship with that first human. We cannot share our minds with land animals or birds as we can share with one another. Jesus calls the disciples friends when he can tell them, and they can know, what he is doing and why, which is to say, he calls them friends when they are able with intimate mutual understanding to love one another even unto death. Friendship entails greater mutuality than turned out to be possible with animals. Yet it seems that God thought friendship with animals might be possible or at least was worth trying even if it wasn't going to turn out to be possible. Which leads to the second point: none of the animals thereby created was meant to be ruled over by the original human, because that kind of knowledge was not to exist in the world. Thus the aboriginal relationship of human and animal was to be a certain sort of companionship that, while lacking the equality and full sharing that mark friendship, was nonetheless free of any sort of dominion. We might say that the vision of man and beast in Genesis 2 was of friendliness. If in some way unforeseen by the canonical text it should develop that we, humans and animals, might become full friends with one another, that would be a good thing.[5]

Genesis 2 gives an account of why we are not friends with birds and beasts. (It is different from Genesis 1, wherein the plural human beings were made to dominate all other creatures.) And thus Genesis 2 holds within itself the thought that in another world, perhaps even in the kingdom of heaven, such friendship might exist. In the Harry Potter books, one finds mythical animals that have rationality and could possibly be friends with humans if the opportunities and prejudices were ever worked out (see the thestrals above; see also the haughty centaurs). In *The Lord of the Rings*, Gandalf shares his mind with Gwaihir, a great Eagle, who cooperates in the quest and might well be thought of as a trans-species friend of his, along with

Aragorn and Elrond. C. S. Lewis' Narnia is also a land where animals and humans can share with one another and grow to have that common mind in common action that characterizes true friendship. But those illustrations come from the world of fantasy. In the world as it is, are there any nonhuman created beings with whom we might be friends? To look for such a friend is to look for a neighbor. Oliver O'Donovan explains that the "neighbor" (as in "Thou shalt love thy neighbor as thyself") is one who is given alongside us in the world to love. A neighbor is someone like me and so cannot be "out there" the way I might know and love something else (a symphony, a sunset, a forest). This beside-me-yet-not-me is what reveals the neighbor as my potential friend, for both my neighbor and my friend will be someone who is like me while yet remaining other.[6] The archetype of both neighbor and friend is given in Genesis 2: the woman and the man see each other and recognize that *this* other could have been me and yet is irreducibly other. A dog, an eagle, a lion, a sparrow—while these are irreducibly other, they could never have been me, not in the world as it is. But the neighbor is closer; she could have been me.

A progressive thread that runs through history is the discovery of others we did not previously know existed but who we came to see were our neighbors and thus people with whom we could be friendly and might become friends. When Europeans discovered (what we now call) the Indigenous peoples of the Americas at the end of the fifteenth century, such occurred, not at once but upon theological reflection. Francisco de Vitoria (c. 1483–1546), for an important example, saw the Indigenous peoples (whom he called Indians) as potential Christians who were to be neither forced to convert nor exploited. They were, however, human beings with whom we could have conversation and share the gospel with reason and miracle.[7] With them, we could become friends. Another instance, from a couple of centuries later, is Abbé Charles-Michel de l'Épée (1712–89), who recognized the humanity of deaf children as manifested in their ability to communicate. He set out to educate them for the sake of their flourishing as human beings; not incidentally, that education opened for them the possibility of receiving the sacraments. He recognized their capacity for friendship.

Sometimes people wonder about the possibility of nonhuman rational beings living elsewhere in the universe. If we were to discover them, they would be, like the Indigenous peoples, neighbors: beings alongside us. That is to say, they might become our friends; we could, at least in principle, come to share a common mind. This is not to underestimate the difficulties and the manifold possibilities of misunderstanding. But it does show that neighbor, like brother or sister, and like friend, need not be someone who is a potential sexual partner. This also is why, by the way, there is no need for the Word of God to be incarnate on every planet that has rational beings: what he did on earth is for everyone—an insight built into C. S. Lewis' space trilogy, especially *Perelandra*.[8]

Clones: *Never Let Me Go*

In a book seminar we were discussing *Never Let Me Go*, the haunting, award-winning 2005 novel by Kazuo Ishiguro.[9] The author conjures an alternative present, a world in which a number of diseases have been eliminated thanks to the availability of organs from clones. The truth of the situation is only gradually made clear to the reader, who discovers it from inside the thoughts of one of the clones, Kathy H. (she has no last name), who is now thirty-one and trying to make sense of her life before she comes to the end of it. We find that she had been part of a humane effort, now abandoned, to improve the clones' lives by giving these children education and encouraging their artistic abilities. The movers behind the effort were trying to demonstrate to society at large that the clones had souls, that they were capable of emotions and thoughts just like the rest of us.

As it is easy to imagine, vested interests—in the availability of organs, in the conquering of disease—were far too strong to be overturned by quibbles over the ethics of the project. In their world, certain diseases had been eliminated! If we started questioning where the replacement organs came from, what would be the point? We can't go back on this important medical-scientific achievement!

Hauntingly for us who read it, the novel shows these children (and then young adults) as, apart from their infertility, quite ordinarily human: they have crushes; they have hopes; they try to understand what other people are thinking; they are curious about the world. We see them live lives that are largely insulated from those of normal humans. For obvious reasons, the project requires that they have as little contact as possible with the rest of the world. Although dwelling in the midst of the same country as everyone else, they live in special homes (one senses, often shabby). They make their "donations" and ultimately "complete" (the euphemism for their final, fatal donation) in a world that benefits from them and provides for them, to the extent it does, with as little interaction as possible.

For there is near-universal revulsion toward them, although the humane project that Kathy H. was a part of involved people who worked to overcome that. Revulsion is understandable of course. These—what do we say? "children"? "people"?—had been brought into existence only to provide organs for donation; after a few donations, they will complete. To allow oneself to touch such a being—to allow oneself to teach, even to care for, such a being—was taboo, unthinkable.

Ishiguro brings us to see that there are some experiments that we should never begin. To bring into being copies of people merely for the advantage of others is a lethal assault on our humanity. Yet let us suppose, with the novel, that such an experiment has been done, that these instrumentalized people have come into existence. Here they are, like us in every way except for their engineered infertility. They are just as individual, just as really human, as any person reading these words. In the novel, they are beside the people of England and yet not beside them, they are neighbors and yet not neighbors. To repeat, what haunts the reader is their humanity, which we see above all in their friendships with one another. It just simply is the case: they are capable of friendship in the ordinary ways children and young adults are. Sometimes they think of what the other would want. They try to understand each other's feelings and thoughts. The narrator, particularly, has been a good "carer" for nearly a dozen years because of her ability to be with and help others as they "donate." Yet she also wants us to know she isn't particularly special. The reader gets the point: they all are capable, as capable as I and thou, of sharing thoughts and feelings and adventures and work. Their lives are much abbreviated, and yet they do not lack this.

Could they be friends with us? That, it turns out, is the most important question of all. Their existence is a contradiction in the midst of the alternative-present of the book, for if we were to refuse to touch them—if we allowed our revulsion to keep us from opening ourselves to them—then we would have denied our own humanity.

Jesus, one remembers (although he is entirely absent from this book), turned the question of neighbor upside down, asking not "Who is my neighbor?" but rather "Who proved himself to be a neighbor?" So is it here. The real question is not whether they could be friends with us but whether we would be friends with them.

Further Thoughts on the Difference between Sex and Friendship

The question of whether we can be a friend with another being is importantly different from the question of whether another being is human like us. One test that has been put forth for whether other beings are human is whether we can procreate with them. A novel from 1953 by Vercors, the pen name of Jean Bruller, who was called "the literary backbone of the [French] Resistance" during the Second World War, postulates the discovery of hitherto unknown beings in a remote place who might be ape-like humans or who might be human-like apes. On which side of the human-animal divide do they fall? The protagonist, who was part of their discovery, is dismayed by the social and financial powers who wish to profit from these beings and put them in zoos. Persuaded that they are human, he sets out to prove it. He fathers a child by one of them and then kills the child—and then summons the police and insists on being jailed for murder. If convicted, as he hopes, his case would provide judicial evidence that these beings are human and cannot be treated as property.[10]

But just as friendship is a broader category than marriage, so does it extend beyond those with whom we could potentially have children. It would extend, as Ishiguro urges us to see, to technologically engineered beings who are infertile; it would certainly also extend to clones and other human-created human beings who were potentially fertile. It would extend, were they to exist, to intelligent animals with whom we might take counsel and pursue common enterprises, animals such as the Eagles in Tolkien and the centaurs in Rowling.

A few pages above, I broached the question of extending friendship even to an extraterrestrial. The idea is remote and strange, and yet, if in this universe, created and sustained by God, there is life elsewhere with which we might communicate, such life cannot be beyond the possible reach of friendship. In this regard, I have enjoyed Mary Doria Russell's *The Sparrow* as a science-fiction novel about the discovery of intelligent extraterrestrial life and a privately financed mission (involving the Jesuits!) to meet them. Profound misunderstanding ensues, as the extraterrestrial life is itself a complex and compromised social mix. Nonetheless, one sees the possibilities of friendship developing, with extremely high risks both to the people from earth and to those beings they visit.[11]

To push even further, could humans ever become friends with some form of artificial intelligence? Might a robot be my friend? As long as there is nothing in the robot apart from what we have put there, it seems not. In *Ready Player One*, the narrator, Wade, lives in a virtual reality world through his avatar, Parzival. He has an assistant, Max, for whom he has written code that creates a personality. When feeling down, Wade can talk with Max and have his mind taken off his problems—until Max starts repeating himself. That painfully reminds Wade that there is no more to Max than what he, Wade, has created.[12]

But what if we got cleverer than that? What if we made a device that was then able to replicate itself—a computer, say, that could go around and pick up various bits of the world and make another computer, which itself also had the capacity to make another, and so on? Herbert McCabe says that such a thing would be alive, which is to say, we should describe it as having a soul. (A soul is not a thing a body has but rather the "form" of a living body. When a body dies, it loses its form—which we will see if we wait a bit; decomposition will become evident.)

We might well hesitate at the metaphysics of ascribing a soul to a machine with artificial intelligence, but would we necessarily be in error to start thinking of such a machine as a potential friend? Perhaps—as with an extraterrestrial, the difficulties of mutual understanding could be enormous. They might be insurmountable. In the 2014 film *Ex Machina*, a man falls in love with a sensuous robot who returns his love, or seems to until the point that he arranges her escape. She then departs the compound and without a word, without a glance, leaves him behind—locked up and apparently doomed to starve to death. Is this an intrinsic defect of AI—that true friendship will be impossible? Or is it merely another instance of sinful manipulation of others in a fallen world? At the least, the film certainly succeeds as a moral tale on the importance of not mistaking sexual pleasure for friendship!

The Horizon of Friendship

The most important task of moral development is to grow in friendship. We learn how to do this and take encouragement from examples, from simple experiences to far-out speculations. Although this chapter's survey is admittedly idiosyncratic, it has aimed to show, through a variety of friendships real and imagined, that friendship has an internal dynamic of expansion. It is a desire for intimacy—in its clearer forms, for nonsexual intimacy—that seeks to be at once deep and wide. From the scriptural story of our ancient origins to science-inspired speculative tales of our future, we find humans desiring friendship and wondering, *Whom else might I be friends with?* That question is behind the animals of Genesis 2, as it is behind movements against slavery and racism. It is behind, if only so tentatively, contemporary cultural desires to have friends rather than only sexual partners, friends who last, friends who are good to the end, like Frodo and Sam, little people whose intimate friendship is forged in the struggle for the good and joined thereby for all time with such big people as the elf Elrond, the man Aragon, the wizard Gandalf, and even great Eagles.

Who else might join in our friendship?

ELEVEN

All Together Now

Friendship with God: The Final Frontier to Which Job Points

I am on record (in *Losing Susan*) as saying that the second-best book of the Bible is the Song of Songs. It is a deep exploration of how sexual longing is a fitting way to speak of the love of humans and God for each other. The late theologian Robert Jenson shows (you can find the details of the argument throughout his commentary)[1] that the literal meaning of the text (the meaning intended by the author) just is the allegorical meaning. (In many places, the surface story breaks down into incoherence.) If sexual longing can serve such a high function as to be a way for us to speak of the mutual love of God for us and us for him, then there is nothing intrinsically wrong with it. The arguments of the book in your hands—that marriage is the context for human sexual intimacy; that marriage is a form of friendship; that friendship, in this way unlike marriage, is natively expansive; that our human fulfillment does not require sexual intimacy but does require the development and deepening of friendships—none of these would gainsay the beautiful truths of the second-best book of the Bible. Indeed, one could see the Song of Songs as the culmination of the line of thought about loving God and God loving us—a line of thought that, as we have seen, is very slow to emerge in the Bible and yet leads us ultimately to the inner life of God himself.

However, I am also on record (also in *Losing Susan*) as holding that the best book of the Bible is the book of Job. In chapter 6 above, we saw how Job is a book about human friendship; it arguably shows us more about friendship than anything else in the Old Testament. And in other places, we have noticed how divine friendship is a slowly emerging desire: from Abraham (called God's friend because God shared his mind with him) and Moses (who spoke with God as one does with a friend) to its fulfillment in Jesus, who opens such possibility of intimacy with God to all people. Now I want to say more about the book of Job, for in that book, as it turns out, we can see coming together both human and divine friendships in a manner that takes us right up to the verge of the Christian mystery.

First, there is the revelation of true human friendship. We have noted that Job's three friends come to him immediately after his catastrophe; they sit with him in silence, the silent solidarity of friends in the face of evil. Once their conversations with Job begin, they quickly take on an edge; the friends find themselves offended; their speeches fail of mutual comprehension. Yet we should note one thing that does not happen: the friends do not, in a huff, turn away from Job and go away. They persist with him—and he with them. In this imperfect world, finite and mystifying, communications can be difficult. Sometimes friends need to tell us things that we don't want to hear but are good for us. Sometimes friends tell us things that they think we need to hear even though they are not good for us. No words are perfect, no communication perfect, in this world of ours.

Finally, God takes Job on that journey to the wild side. Job sees how full of marvels and powerful and frightening realities the world is; he beholds the world as far bigger and more alien than ever he had thought. As a result of taking up God's invitation, Job takes in how small and yet infinitely precious is the little, protected human world. He, and his friends, and all humanity—it's all just "dust and ashes." And yet it is beautiful. We see that Job realizes this beauty in the names he gives his daughters, names that signify beauty. And we see it in his adjustment, entirely unprecedented, of his last will and testament, in which those daughters will inherit equally alongside their brothers.

Let us summon up one last time that final scene of the book of Job, that tender scene of communion. His friends are there, and his brothers, and his sisters, and all his acquaintances; gifts are brought and food is eaten. And they all comfort Job "over all the evil that the LORD had brought upon him" (Job 42:11). But let us note: they do not shake their fists at the Lord. They are not angry with God; they do not curse (as Satan wrongly predicted Job would). They simply accept that evils may come upon us from the Lord, who, in his confoundedly mysterious way, has made a universe in which such things happen. The Lord is responsible for what has happened to Job. But he is also responsible for Leviathan—and he has provided a corner of the universe where human beings can live together, and be friends.

This final scene takes us, I say, right up to the gospel. It shows us the accomplishment of human friendship, which is the work of the incarnation of Jesus, who on the eve of his death says, "I have called you friends." Jesus makes friendship. But there is more.

Job wanted to speak to God "man to man," to put it in old-fashioned terms. He wanted to address God with dignity, as an equal, not as a child addresses a parent and certainly not as a poverty-stricken, impecunious, boil-covered, tiny subject might address the king of his realm. He wanted to talk. In the online mercantile world, we know the frustrations of that anonymity of addressee: an electronic transaction goes wrong, and we click all over the website to try to find some way to get through to someone, some way to make a contact. We want someone to talk to! Job wanted that—with God. He did not call it friendship, but he wanted it.

When finally God does speak to Job, he says, in effect, "You wanted to speak to me? Here I am; let's have some Q&A." God appears in awe and power, although also with that sense of saying, "Please, let's have this conversation." The conversation points not only to the wild awesomeness of the vast universe beyond Job's ken but also to their inequality. Job and God are not on the same level. Some wit has summarized the book of Job as saying, "I'm God and you're not." That certainly is in the mix of things.

Yet before the catastrophe comes upon Job, and again at the end, there is communication with God in the form of prayer. Both at the beginning and at the end, Job in the role of an intercessor turns to God. It is almost the first thing we learn in the book, that Job regularly offers early morning sacrifices for his sons (in case, in their customary feasting, they have "sinned, and cursed God in their hearts" [Job 1:5]).[2] And at the end of the book, he offers prayer for his friends. This latter prayer, significantly, is done after the Lord speaks directly to Eliphaz concerning his speech and that of the other two friends: "Ye have not spoken of me the thing that is right, as my servant Job hath" (42:7). The Lord is displeased with what they have said about him. But we should not fail to see that *the Lord actually speaks, and speaks directly, not only to Job but also to Eliphaz.* Not only does Job get the satisfaction of his desire to hear the Lord speak to him, but that desire of Job's is fulfilled also for Eliphaz. What was it that was wrong with what Eliphaz and the others had said about God? Was their mis-speech about God as bad as cursing God in their hearts (which, at the beginning, Job feared his sons might have done)? This seems unlikely. How then had they failed to speak "the thing that is right"? Could it be that they never desired God to speak to them?

The final scene of the book, that communion in Job's home with his friends and brothers and sisters, all his acquaintances, with their eating and their gift giving and their commiseration—that warm, homely communion—comes about only because Job was willing to pray (and did pray) for his friends. Job's prayer is a seed pregnant not only with the restoration of human friendship but with the establishment of divine friendship as well. Job prays and thus talks with God, who has talked with him. Job prays among others for Eliphaz, who failed to speak truly about God and to whom God nonetheless also spoke. With his prayer at the end, we have the profoundest sense in which Job takes us to friendship—to divine friendship, the final frontier of the gospel.

For when Jesus shares his mind with his disciples, the content of his sharing is everything he has received from the Father. Jesus, being at once fully God and fully human, can give grace (the Holy Spirit) to his disciples whereby they are lifted up to a level equal with God. If the disciples are no longer, thanks to Jesus' death, merely his disciples but fully friends with him who laid down his life for them, then they are also by that very fact friends of God.

This is not yet manifest in Job, but we can see it as the frontier to which Job has led us up. It is the case, as Robert Jenson used to teach us, that the Triune God is present throughout the Old Testament.[3] He is the creator who gives everything existence for as long as it exists. But he has also, always, wanted to be with his creation, to be among them, in a pillar of fire, in a cloud, on a mercy seat. And he is through it all, also, the wind that blows history along, the Spirit whose guarantee is that there is a future of meaningfulness for us, that at the end, our lives will not turn out to signify nothing.

The God of the Old Testament is the Triune identity of Christian faith, but in the Old Testament, he has not yet effectuated friendship with human beings at large. That takes his incarnation, his becoming a character in the story, one of us, full stop. It requires that Jesus' life be fulfilled in death, offered as the high moment in which friendship is sealed. Job, it seems to me, wanted precisely this, even if he lacked the words for it. He wanted not just to speak to God as in a court, not just to speak to God as a legal opponent, but to speak to God as a friend.

The Two Aspects of Friendship with God

What does it mean for God to be our friend? This question requires two answers, each of them necessary. It will not be clear how the two answers hold together logically. But the testimony of countless Christians is that, like the two natures in the one divine person of Jesus Christ, these two answers can be held together in an integral human life.

The first answer is that we know God in his awesome otherness, in his power. This powerful God is the creator of the ever-expanding interstellar spaces in which any of us would instantly die. He is the power beneath volcanoes. He made Leviathan. If I may speak personally, he created Susan, gave her to me as my wife, and then took her away. Also personally, Job could say that he gave him his children and wealth and community prestige and practical wisdom—and then took it all away, covering his body with boils. But there is more to this first answer. God, as we know him in this awe-ful-ness, is also, we can see, not indifferent to us. He knows us; and however inchoately, we grasp that his intentions to us are not malevolent—which is to say, Job may not grasp how God is good, but he knows he is not evil.

So, first, we know God as benevolent power. But second, to be God's friend means we also know him as, in some way, our equal. We are not equal to God as creatures—Job can have no answer when God asks, "Where wast thou when I laid the foundations of the earth?" (Job 38:4). Rather, equality comes to us by grace, by God's pure gift. God wants to be our friend, and so he makes it possible by lifting us up to his level of being. This grace is the gift of God's Spirit.

And the result is quite ordinary. It means we can talk to God, and he can talk to us, just as we would talk to anyone else.

Grace

Here is how I start my days, now that I'm coming to the end of this book. I rise about five o'clock and make some tea. I read Morning Prayer, often going very slowly through the Psalms and the assigned Old Testament reading in particular. If I find I'm not paying attention (which often happens), I go back and read again. About 5:30 I turn to a theological book that I am studying and read it closely for another half hour. Then I go for a run, just a mile or so (I'm an old guy) down an urban trail where there used to be train tracks. There's a coffee house at the end of my run. I take my journal with me, and with a "tall bold" and a cup of water, I write.

I write to God. I tell him what the temperature is, what I'm wearing, how my body feels, when I got up, what I did yesterday, what's on my mind, and so forth. Sometimes I pose questions to him. And the way he talks to me is very ordinary. It's just what a good friend would do. He shows me back myself, helps me see who I am. He may bring something to mind, give me a thought I hadn't had before. He can open a horizon, offer an insight into other people, give me a task. Or sometimes he just reminds me of simple truths that are pertinent to the moment. If I'm anxious, he might put me in mind of his sovereignty over the future. "Victor, this is what you can do today. Let's put off thinking about next week or next year!" He makes me smile at myself.

It has taken me a while to get to this point, but I no longer try to hide my sins from my journal. It's more important for me to write to God about them than to worry about what a future reader may think. (Dear future reader, pray for me, and if I seem an awful person, pray for me all the more.) As I write to God with such openness as I can, he helps me understand myself more truthfully. Even when uncomfortable, self-knowledge is a good thing, particularly when offered by a friend.

When my coffee is gone, I wrap up and run back home, and the day begins. God is with me through the day, and I try to remember that. He's a very good friend. He never misunderstands me, though I often misunderstand myself. He's never preoccupied. Presence, tenderness, clarity, truth, love—these are always there.

The danger with this sort of friendship practice is that it can turn Jesus into merely a chum—what might be called an emphasis on his humanity at the expense of his divinity. That's why our friendship also needs practices that bring to mind the awe-ful power of God, which is of course fully present in Jesus. This one to whom I can write familiarly is also the one who holds me in being. Indeed, I might even write that. *You give me life and breath. You are like a hand wrapped around my beating heart. You can command the tsunami to stop. You give and you take away. There is no end to your power and strength and mystery. And nonetheless, you also love me and let me write to you as if we were simply friends.*

Which we are, and into which, please God, may we grow forever.

Postscript

Concrete Practices

How to Practice Friendship

These are suggestions—nothing more—that try to capture the practical side of the reflections in this book and yours truly's own experience. You should feel free to modify them. In fact, you *should* modify them. The most important step is to take to heart the truth that friendship is the point of being human. Then ask God to lead you to that fulfillment. All the rest are details—variable practices that are subject to change. With that in mind, I suggest the following.

1. *Identify the true friends you have.* These will be a few people, at least three and probably no more than six, who are (or you sense might become) your friends in the primary sense of the word, whose friendship is based on the good you see in each other, the good you draw out in each other, the good you see and wish to promote in the world, and the good you find in God. (If you are married, one of these friends is likely your spouse.) Pray for them daily, and give thanks to God that he has given you them. Contact them regularly. If you can't meet with them, speak with them by telephone at least monthly for enough time to share your lives and to hear their "living voice." Meet with them face to face whenever possible; it seems to me that a personal annual visit is the minimum. Seek to do things with them (meals, projects, exercises, events, and so on). Enjoy their company and with them seek the good. Hold each other to high but

realistic standards, yet do so encouragingly. If one of your friends tells you something about yourself that is hard to hear, thank her and take it to heart; this doesn't mean that you need to agree but rather that you will seriously consider it. Talk with each other about God, about love, about the things in the world that are good. Be sure to talk sometimes about friendship itself, not in an inward-turning way but in a way that opens you and your friend to embrace the world. Any true friendship will open out into the world—will reach for the good. Or it may already be situated there; you might well have become friends because you were together engaged in a common project (at work, play, church, or elsewhere). Remember that the time you spend on and with your friends is the most important time in the world.

2. *Keep old friends in mind.* You have former friends, people you used to be close to but who, for some reason, have fallen away. This need not be a concern. Of course, if there was a harm done or some sort of sin that caused the separation, then you should identify it and repent, as we have learned as Christians to do. But generally, you have former friends because of happenstance—as happens when someone moves to a new city. Realize that such former friends remain friends, even though your friendship is not presently being actualized. Such a friendship is "on hold." Pray for them whenever you think of them, commending them to God's ongoing care. But do not feel guilty that you lack the time to keep these friendships going. We are finite beings. God's promise is that in his fullness these friendships will be enjoyed again. Look forward to that day, and in the meantime, if it happens that you can do something for a former friend, then do so.

3. *Be open to new friends, even as you seek to deepen the friendships you have.* When the kingdom comes in its fullness, the salvation that Jesus has wrought will be consummated in a universal friendship embracing all his friends. We cannot yet imagine how that will be. But we can anticipate it in the concrete expectation that God always intends to give us a new friend, and then another. So when you find yourself drawn to someone, consider whether God might be offering him or her to you as a new friend. It might not be so—friendship takes serious time and commitment—but it might be so. You should aim neither to make friends too quickly (for that prevents you from

the depth that friendship needs) nor to avoid making new friends (perhaps out of fear or tiredness or complacency).

4. *Aim to have friendly relations with the many other people in your life.* Insofar as you can, learn their names. Show yourself glad to see them. Appreciate what each of you brings to the common life. I am thinking here of coworkers, neighbors, relatives, store clerks, bus drivers, doctors—all the people you meet on your daily walk. As Oliver O'Donovan puts it, when we are friendly with someone, we are saying that although we are not actually friends, if it should turn out in God's good time that we were to become friends, that would be "no bad thing."[1] Which is to say again that you have a place in your heart that is open to having more friends, and you would be glad for that circle of friends to expand again and again. Our being friendly is a way of showing our readiness for that future consummation, when all the friends of Jesus will be the friends of all the friends of Jesus.

5. *Love every human being, as our Lord bids us.* In our present life, this Christian love must be distinguished from friendship. Unlike friendship, universal Christian love does not discriminate between the good and the bad, and it does not look for reciprocity. It does not overshare; it holds back from inappropriate openness. It is, as it were, a friendliness that extends to the unfriendly. It is not friendship, because it is unidirectional; it is not intimate sharing. Nonetheless, it is an offer. To your enemies, to people who seem to you to be on a wicked path, indeed (if it were possible so to judge) to people who really are committed to wickedness, you are still to offer love. This takes such concrete forms as a basic respect of human dignity, a recognition of a common humanity in another person, a desire to prove yourself a neighbor when that is possible (again recognizing human finitude). You should pray for your enemies, that God would turn their hearts to him. When Christ's kingdom comes in its fullness, there will be no difference between this universal human love and friendship: it is a distinction necessitated only by the persistence of sin in this in-between time. So in this meantime, do some concrete works of charity in your life. Indeed, talk over with your friends what concrete works you can join in together. That too is a way to prepare the ground for the spread of friendship.

How to Practice Friendship with God

Again, these are nothing more than suggestions.

1. *Read some Scripture daily, directly encountering it.* If you turn
to a commentary for help, go back from that commentary to the
text. I repeat the point, because nothing can take its place: directly
encounter the text. Have a plan for doing so, at least an initial plan
(e.g., to read for fifteen minutes each morning from Saint Matthew).
A lectionary can be a good guide; there are also schemes for reading
the Bible through in a year. You may find that when you finish a book
(e.g., Matthew), you want to go back and start it again. Do so! Ask
God to fill your heart with a longing to be familiar with his written
Word. Seek to understand God's character. Seek above all for him
to show you his strange friendship, that although he is the creator
of the world, he loves it and gave his life to establish friendship with
you (and me and uncountable others).

2. *Daily communicate with God as with a friend.* Imagine Jesus
is right beside you. What do you want to say to him? Say it—or, as I
do presently, write it. Or draw a picture for him. You need dedicated
time for this, and it should be every day. I think fifteen minutes is
minimal. Friendship takes time—a truth that applies to friendship
with God as much as any other friendship. Many of us feel that our
lives are too busy, that we don't have time for friendship. I suspect
everyone feels that at times. But friendship should not be sacrificed
for other busyness. Your daily talking with God needs to be informal.
It needs to be in your own words. It needs to be honest. It can include
anything, from a foot that's hurting, to a child who's in trouble, to
a problem at work, to financial desires or worries. It can of course
include talk about sex. It must include talk about things that embar-
rass you, or attract you, or make you happy. The point is intimacy:
nothing should be excluded from your conversation with this friend.

3. *Talk with God about your friendship with him.* Perhaps, like
me, you have wondered how Jesus can be your truest friend of all.
There is of course no competition between real friends: friends are
not jealous of one another but rejoice in sharing their love with new
friends. Yet with all my other friends, I can, for instance, share a hug,
their voices can enter my ear, and so on. So I ask Jesus, "How are you

my friend?" He talks with me in prayer, and he gives me himself in Communion. But still I can't look into his eyes. So I tell him, "I long to see your eyes." Expressing this longing is an important practice of friendship with God.

4. *Find opportunities in your life to experience the transcendence of God, his power, his awesomeness, his beauty.* This might mean visiting a grand church when you can, kneeling, staring, smelling. It might happen in your Sunday worship. Some people climb mountains. Others listen for birds. Some are just suddenly caught, as they walk, by bright berries on a bush. In Marilynne Robinson's novel *Gilead*, John Ames sits in the silence of a simple church, waiting for the sun to rise.[2] The one who holds all this in being offers each of us the chance to be lifted out of ourselves. You need to find these divine invitations to be still and know he is God.

5. *Try to think about God throughout the day.* Try to offer short prayers whenever there is a space for them in your life. Ask God to remind you that he is always with you. This, I think, is the meaning of praying always. Your friend is always with you. Indeed, in these little prayers, you may sense the difference you make to Jesus. You might hear him say, "I like the way you're doing that" or "Do you see how you've helped this person?"—which is to say, you might get a glimpse of how you are pleasing him (in addition, of course, to the important self-knowledge that comes from our sins). Keeping your friend in mind throughout the day is one concrete way to see how divine friendship has both giving and receiving.

6. *Look for ways to become cognizant of this great mystery: not only do we desire to be a friend with God, but God himself also desires to be a friend with us.* The awesome truth is that the longing goes two ways. Not only do you want him but he also wants you. (Remember the Song of Songs!) Consider the bread and wine of the Holy Table. This is his gift to you of himself, a true sign of his longing to be one with you. He wants, even as we want, for him to dwell in us and us in him.

7. *Let your life be full of thanksgiving.* Thank God daily most especially for the friends he has given you. Let him know that even as you are glad to be his friend now, you also look forward to that great day of sharing in his friendship with all his friends.

Credits and Acknowledgments

"BCP" refers to the Episcopal Church's 1979 Book of Common Prayer. Page numbers are kept constant across various editions and publishers. Although there have been changes to the minor commemorations and the lectionary since its initial publication, none of these have changed the pagination or other content of the book.

The quotation from the Rev. Andrew C. Mead's sermon at the funeral of John Scott is printed with his kind permission.

Portions of a chapter on friendship in my *Christian Ethics: A Guide for the Perplexed* (London: Bloomsbury T&T Clark, 2012) appear here and there in revised form in this book with the kind permission of the publisher.

Drafts of various parts of this book were developed from the Muhlenberg Lenten Lectures delivered at the Parish of Calvary–St. George's in New York City and from talks and lectures given at All Souls' Church in Oklahoma City; the Church of St. Michael and St. George in St. Louis; the Cathedral Church of St. Matthew in Dallas; Church of the Incarnation in Dallas; Trinity Cathedral in Columbia, South Carolina; and at Canterbury House, Dallas, under the sponsorship of the Living Church Institute. I am grateful for the hospitality and opportunities for discussion that the clergy and people of these congregations and foundations gave me.

In thinking through this matter of friendship, I enjoyed countless conversations with people, more than I can possibly remember.

Indeed, if you and I have ever talked, you have entered somehow into this book. I have discovered that people are eager to talk about friendship and that everyone has some measure of understanding along with real questions. To everyone who has talked with me, my thanks. There are, however, two people whom I cannot leave behind the curtain of anonymity. First is Wesley Hill, whose early and wise encouragement, not to mention his book *Spiritual Friendship* and the blog of that name, has given me ongoing insight and hope. The other is my granddaughter Lucy, who at the end of her first decade of life is already quite clear that friends help us be better, and when we disagree, that is not necessarily a bad thing. Friendship is about the good, it leads us to the good, and it is good.

Notes

Invocation

1. Prayer adapted from "O Worship the King," hymn by Robert Grant.

Introduction

1. The direct Psalm quotation is from the Episcopal Church's 1979 Book of Common Prayer (hereafter BCP). Verse numbers in this Psalter do not always correspond to canonical numbers. See Book of Common Prayer (New York: Church Publishing, 1979).

2. BCP, 333.

3. The irrepressible Malcolm Guite once told the clergy of the Episcopal Diocese of Dallas that if we wanted to think about what poetry is, we should skip "middle management" and go straight to Shakespeare.

Chapter 1 The Limits of Marriage

1. "In the kingdom . . . when the love of God for mankind is fully revealed . . . there will be no God in the sense of what is set above or apart from man. God will simply be the life of mankind." Herbert McCabe, "Freedom," in *God Matters* (London: Geoffrey Chapman, 1987), 24. Add to this the following, from the same volume: "Jesus was the first human being, the first member of the human race in whom humanity came to fulfilment, the first human being for whom to live was simply to love. . . . The aim of human life is to live in friendship—a friendship amongst ourselves which in fact depends on a friendship, or covenant, that God has established between ourselves and him" ("Good Friday," 93).

Chapter 2 The Confusions of Friendship

1. A third and shorter work, the *Magna Moralia*, seems to follow the *Eudemian* but with "a number of misunderstandings of its doctrine"; Anthony Kenny supposes

it to consist of student notes. See Aristotle, *The Eudemian Ethics*, trans. and intro. Anthony Kenny (Oxford: Oxford University Press, 2011), x–xii.

2. These parenthetical notations direct the reader to the page and line in the standard Greek text and can be found in the margins of most translations. A single reference at the end of a paragraph pertains to all the direct quotations within the paragraph. All translations of the *Eudemian Ethics* herein are from Kenny.

3. Of course, once a child becomes an adult, the two can become peers and then, quite possibly, friends in the primary sense. This would not be inconsistent with Aristotle's thought, nor would a similar development into equality in a marriage (which Aristotle takes as fundamentally unequal) or in some other initially unequal pairing, however exceptional that development would be.

Chapter 3 Friendship as Success at Being Human

1. Herbert McCabe refers to the "creation question" as a question "asked by the Jews, at least from Second Isaiah onwards, the question which, once asked, could not be unasked." Herbert McCabe, "The Involvement of God," in *God Matters* (London: Geoffrey Chapman, 1987), 42.

2. See William Lane Craig, *The Kalam Cosmological Argument* (New York: Barnes and Noble Books, 1979).

3. Consider: If your age were infinite, how old were you five hundred years ago? Infinite again, because if you take five hundred away from infinity, you still have infinity. The paradoxical conclusion is that if you are actually infinitely old, you never were five years old, or fifty, or five hundred, or . . . Thus while we can imagine always becoming a year older, never dying, without end, we cannot jump from that to being actually infinite in age.

4. McCabe, "Creation," in *God Matters*, 6.

5. I use masculine pronouns for God only out of humility before tradition. Our discomfort with them is a recognition of the breaking down of language when we speak of God. But the alternatives (feminine or neuter pronouns, or the avoidance of pronouns altogether) are no better, and they can mislead us into thinking we have rectified an error.

6. All quotations from the *Lysis* are from the 1910 translation of J. Wright as revised and published in Edith Hamilton and Huntington Cairns, eds., *The Collected Dialogues of Plato*, Bollingen Series LXXI (Princeton: Princeton University Press, 1961 [corrected ed. 1963]). For Edith Hamilton's introduction to the *Lysis*, see *Collected Dialogues*, 145. Parenthetical notations in the text are made conventionally to the standard Stephanus page and page subdivision, as found in the margins of most translations.

7. See Mark Vernon, *The Philosophy of Friendship* (Basingstoke, UK; New York: Palgrave Macmillan, 2005). In an appendix, Vernon deftly compares Aristotle and Plato, with an insightful reading of the *Lysis*.

8. When I speak of the Socratic method or of Socrates himself, I am not making any distinction between Socrates the man who taught Plato and Socrates the character in Plato's dialogues. I am also running together Socrates' teaching and Plato's. In both cases, scholars explore fascinating, subtle differences, which are, however, beyond the scope of this book.

9. The word *philosophers* within brackets is in Hamilton and Cairns.

Chapter 4 Friendship and Beauty

1. Elaine Scarry, *On Beauty and Being Just* (Princeton: Princeton University Press, 1999), 6.
2. "How to Make Friends? Study Reveals Time It Takes," University of Kansas, March 28, 2018, https://news.ku.edu/2018/03/06/study-reveals-number-hours-it-takes-make-friend.
3. Cicero, *De Senectute, De Amicitia, De Divinationei*, trans. William Armistead Falconer, Loeb Classical Library (1923; repr., Cambridge, MA: Harvard University Press; London: William Heinemann, 1964), 104, 106. In what follows, parenthetical notations in the text refer to this edition.
4. The reader's mind naturally returns to the definition of friendship given by Laelius at the outset in chaps. iv and vi.
5. Here Laelius seems to contradict what he said earlier in chaps. xii–xiii, but the context makes it clear that he is considering not a friend who is moving away from virtue but one who is moving toward virtue but not yet there. In my view, this is just about everyone. One might also consider that in the earlier chapters Laelius was particularly thinking of treason, which here remains something one would not do for a friend, as being a signal instance of "utter disgrace."

Chapter 5 The Weirdness of Divine Love

1. This translation is from Walter M. Abbott, ed., *The Documents of Vatican II* (New York: America Press, 1966), 220, emphasis added. The Latin original is given in Norman P. Tanner, ed., *Decrees of the Ecumenical Councils* (London: Sheed & Ward, 1990), 2:1081: "Reapse noonisi in mysterio Verbi incarnati mysterium hominis vere clarescit. Adam enim, primus homo, erat figura futuri, scilicet Christi domini. Christus, novissimus Adam, in ipsa revelatione mysterii Patris euisque amoris, hominem ipsi homini plene manifestat eique altissimam eius vocationem patefacit."
2. In the Tanner volume, "hominem ipsi homini plene manifestat" is translated as "fully discloses humankind to itself" (2:1081). But "humankind" is a collective that falls short of presenting the entirety of *homo* as an individual *homo*. The desire for inclusive language is commendable, but it can create new problems of its own. Paul and *Gaudium et spes* are concerned to hold before us not "humankind" but two powerful individual men, Adam and Christ, in each of whom every human being is found.
3. The Revised Standard Version (RSV) lacks the definite article; it has "sin which clings so closely," which is more clearly a claim to be about all sin and not just a certain type of sin. By contrast, the King James (Authorized) Version avoids the image of sin as stuck onto us, making it instead something that comes against us: "the sin which doth so easily beset us." For the prayer, see, e.g., BCP, 331.
4. Abbott, *Documents of Vatican II*, 220–21. "Ipse enim, Filius Dei, incarnatione sua cum omni homine quodammodo se univit."
5. See Victor Lee Austin, "John Paul II's Ironic Legacy in Political Theology," *Pro Ecclesia* 16 (2007): 165–94.
6. In all languages, the meanings of words overlap; in Hebrew, various words are translated variously as lover, husband, wife, friend, intimate, fellow citizen, acquaintance, neighbor, companion, associate, another, fellow, even brother and sister, and one word might itself be translated in a number of these ways. A helpful overview

with significant detail is given in the introduction to Saul M. Olyan, *Friendship in the Hebrew Bible* (New Haven: Yale, 2017). The discussion above is not intended to be, nor is the author capable of making, a definitive lexical or textual account. The point is, rather, about the emergence of speech about love and to take note of who is spoken of as the lover and who the beloved.

Chapter 6 Biblical Friendships

1. So Saul M. Olyan: "Although the [Hebrew] word *rēʿa* with the meaning 'friend' and other terms for 'friend' are not used of Jonathan and/or David in the Jonathan-David narratives, the relationship of David and Jonathan is almost universally described as a friendship." Saul M. Olyan, *Friendship in the Hebrew Bible* (New Haven: Yale University Press, 2017), 69.

2. See Robert Alter, *The Art of Biblical Narrative*, rev. ed. (New York: Basic, 2011).

3. While it seems likely to be the case that these two, differing introductions of David indicate redaction from two different sources, it is also the case that the text as we have it can be made sense of—as I hope to be doing in this chapter. See Robert Alter, *The David Story* (New York: Norton, 1999), x: "Much of the richness and complexity of the story is lost by those who imagine this book as a stringing together of virtually independent sources."

4. "This grandly resonant lament . . . is also another public utterance of David's that beautifully serves his political purposes, celebrating his dead rival as it mourns his loss and thus testifying that David could never have desired Saul's death." Alter, *David Story*, note on 2 Sam. 1:17.

5. From the text as we have it, Alter infers that David's "various attachments to women are motivated by pragmatic rather than emotional concerns" or, in the case of Bathsheba, by lust. Alter, *David Story*, note on 2 Sam. 1:26.

6. "Jonathan several times proclaimed his love for David. It is only in Jonathan's death, and at the distance of apostrophe, that David calls him 'my brother' and says that Jonathan was dear to him" (Alter, *David Story*, note on 2 Sam. 1:26). Alter goes on to note that the text "tells us little about David's sexual orientation" and that the bond between warriors, in a warrior culture, "could easily be stronger than the bond between men and women." To my mind, the claim that the Bible points to a homoerotic friendship between David and Jonathan founders on the point that the Bible does not point to it as a friendship.

7. See Robert D. Sacks, *The Book of Job* (Santa Fe, NM: Kafir Yaroq Books, 2016), 250.

8. Sacks translates Job 42:5–6 as follows: "I had heard of you as ears can hear; but now my eyes have seen you. Wherefore I have both contempt and compassion for dust and ashes." Sacks, *Book of Job*, 95.

9. Note that here is a case where the text explicitly says "sisters" as well as "brothers." Even though often in the Scriptures "brethren" is to be taken inclusively, it is important to note the places where the author thought it required explicitly to add "sisters."

10. The sole partial parallel is the daughters of Zelophehad, who inherit after their father's death only because they have no brothers and who are forbidden to marry outside their tribe; Num. 27 and 34. Job's daughters inherit alongside their brothers with no restrictions.

11. The broad lines of this interpretation I owe to Raymond E. Brown, *The Gospel According to John*, vol. 2 (Garden City, NY: Doubleday, 1970).

12. As argues Hans Urs von Balthasar, *Dare We Hope "That All Men Be Saved"?* (San Francisco: Ignatius, 1988).

13. "As it seems to me, the most important thing that Jesus said (and he does not only say it in John's Gospel but shows it and implies it in a thousand ways) is something about himself: that the Father *loves* him." Herbert McCabe, *God Matters* (London: Chapman, 1987; repr., London: Continuum, 2005), 18.

Chapter 7 Christian Friendship and Christian Love

1. This section and the next draw upon and revise elements of the chapter on friendship in Victor Lee Austin, *Christian Ethics: A Guide for the Perplexed* (London: Bloomsbury T&T Clark, 2012).

2. For a valuable and detailed study, see E. D. H. (Liz) Carmichael, *Friendship: Interpreting Christian Love* (London: T&T Clark, 2004).

3. See, for pertinent examples, Carolinne White, *Christian Friendship in the Fourth Century* (Cambridge: Cambridge University Press, 1992), 185.

4. See Joseph Lienhard, "Friendship, Friends," in *Augustine through the Ages: An Encyclopedia*, ed. Allan D. Fitzgerald (Grand Rapids: Eerdmans, 2009), 372–73. Parenthetical notations in the text refer to Saint Augustine, *Confessions*, trans. Henry Chadwick (Oxford: Oxford University Press, 1991).

5. White, *Christian Friendship in the Fourth Century*, chap. 11.

6. As he does, e.g., in *Summa Theologiae* [hereafter ST] II-II.23.1. The move is not wholly without patristic antecedent; see Daniel Schwartz, *Aquinas on Friendship* (Oxford: Clarendon, 2007), 5.

7. The following arguments are indebted to Carmichael, *Friendship*, 105–26.

8. ST II-II.23.1, reply to obj. 2, translation from Saint Thomas Aquinas, *The Summa Theologica*, 2 vols., trans. Fathers of the English Dominican Province, rev. Daniel J. Sullivan, Great Books of the Western World (Chicago: Encyclopaedia Britannica, 1950).

9. Mark F. Williams, trans., "Introduction," *Aelred of Rievaulx's "Spiritual Friendship"* (Scranton, PA: University of Scranton Press, 2002), 10–11.

10. Williams, "Introduction," *Aelred of Rievaulx's "Spiritual Friendship,"* 17.

11. Parenthetical citations are to book and paragraph as noted in Williams' translation; these divisions are from a text established by Anselm Hoste and published in 1971. It is from the Hoste text that Williams has (mostly) translated, and all quotations here are from Williams.

12. Oliver O'Donovan, *Entering into Rest*, vol. 3 of *Ethics as Theology* (Grand Rapids: Eerdmans, 2017), 141.

13. Williams, *Aelred of Rievaulx's "Spiritual Friendship,"* 109n30.

14. For this reading, like that of Job earlier, I have been instructed by Robert D. Sacks, a remarkable and self-effacing tutor emeritus of St. John's College in Santa Fe, New Mexico. See his *Commentary on the Book of Genesis* (Lewiston, NY: Edwin Mellen, 1990). Sacks marshals these additional citations: Gen. 24:50; 31:24, 29; Deut. 1:39; 30:15; 2 Sam. 14:17. "In all these cases the knowledge of good and bad seems to be knowledge appropriate to political life. It has to do with many things. Sometimes, as in the case of Laban, it implies simple power; at other times it concerns free choice

as opposed to prejudices inherited from others. This was the choice which Israel could make only after it had been separated from the Egyptians for forty years." Sacks' reference here is to the change between Deut. 1:39 and 30:15. "Finally, it is the knowledge appropriate to a king" (Sacks, *Commentary on the Book of Genesis*, 29–30). See also Robert D. Sacks, *The Lion and the Ass: Reading Genesis after Babylon* (Santa Fe, NM: Kafir Yaroq Books, 2019), for a well-printed and revised version of this text.

15. Sacks, *Commentary on the Book of Genesis*, 93–114.

16. Williams, *Aelred of Rievaulx's "Spiritual Friendship,"* 108–10, various notes.

17. The adjective is "summa," which O'Donovan translates as "supreme." O'Donovan, *Entering into Rest*, 142.

Chapter 8 Unapologetic Celibacy

1. Augustine, "On the Good of Marriage," 1.1 and 3.3, in Elizabeth Clark, ed., *St. Augustine on Marriage and Sexuality* (Washington, DC: Catholic University of America, 1996), 43, 45.

2. Robert D. Sacks, *Commentary on the Book of Genesis* (Lewiston, NY: Edwin Mellen, 1990), 27.

3. Mark F. Williams, trans., *Aelred of Rievaulx's "Spiritual Friendship"* (Scranton, PA: University of Scranton Press, 2002).

4. Aquinas, rather delightfully, thought that it would be fitting for the resurrected body to be thirty-two or thirty-three years old, which we may think of as the age of Jesus at his death and also roughly the optimal age of the body as we know it: maturity achieved, decline not yet begun. "Those who have not yet come to this [age] have not achieved a perfect state, and older people already have lost it. Therefore to children and to youth [age] is added, but to old folks it is restored." *The Sermon-Conferences of St. Thomas Aquinas on the Apostles' Creed*, trans. Nicholas Ayo (Notre Dame, IN: University of Notre Dame Press, 1988), 147, 149 (in Aquinas' commentary on the resurrection of the flesh).

5. Jonathan Santlofer, *The Widower's Notebook* (New York: Penguin, 2018), 168.

6. There are a growing number of books by Christians trying to think through singleness. I will mention three. (1) Christine A. Colón and Bonnie E. Field, single academic women who had expected that at some point they would be married, focus on the question of celibacy and especially on recovering a positive view of it, particularly in evangelical Christian churches. *Singled Out: Why Celibacy Must Be Reinvented in Today's Church* (Grand Rapids: Brazos, 2009). (2) Jana Marguerite Bennett, a theological ethicist, works through questions of how single Christians could understand desire, perfection, friendship, mission, and more by turning to wisdom from, among others, Paul, Augustine, Wesley, and Aelred. She wants to avoid overemphasizing celibacy and is refreshingly positive about Augustine and Aelred. *Singleness and the Church: A New Theology of the Single Life* (New York: Oxford University Press, 2017). (3) Christina S. Hitchcock, a professor of theology, finds positive content in the lives of single Christians. Their lives testify to both the church and the world about the church (its priority over all other communities), the resurrection (whose reality is the source of Christian identity), and "the proper place for our hope and trust"—namely, the authority of God. Her short and readable book is organized around three figures of that witness: Macrina, Perpetua, and Lottie Moon.

The Significance of Singleness: A Theological Vision for the Future of the Church (Grand Rapids: Baker Academic, 2018).

7. BCP, 423. The 1662 BCP, still the official Book of the Church of England, puts it similarly: "Holy Matrimony . . . is an honorable estate, instituted of God in the time of man's innocency . . . which holy estate Christ adorned and beautified with his presence, and first miracle that he wrought, in Cana of Galilee." The reference to "the time of man's innocency" is absent from the first (1789) U.S. BCP; it appears in the next BCP (1892) but drops out in the 1928 BCP (which has a simple claim that marriage "is an honourable estate, instituted of God"—no mention of innocency or creation and thus silent about whether it might be postlapsarian). In this matter, and also in its articulation of God's intended goods of marriage, the 1979 Book (the current U.S. BCP) recovers an older and more robust teaching. The texts may conveniently be found in Paul V. Marshall, *Prayer Book Parallels*, vol. 1 (New York: Church Hymnal Corporation, 1989), 440–41.

8. This line is not only oft-quoted but also oft-quoted out of context, as toward the end of the film *Call Me by Your Name* when the father uses it to comfort his teenage son at the end of a summer's romance with a man in his twenties. A summer's romance is not a once-in-three-centuries friendship (as Montaigne took his to be)! This quotation (which I have emended) and those that follow are from Michel de Montaigne, *The Complete Essays*, trans. M. A. Screech (London: Penguin, 1991), in which the essay, traditionally titled "On Friendship" but here unfortunately rendered by the translator as "On Affectionate Relationships," is on pages 205–19.

9. Oliver O'Donovan, *Entering into Rest*, vol. 3 of *Ethics as Theology* (Grand Rapids: Eerdmans, 2017), 142.

10. Carol Harrison, "Marriage and Monasticism in St. Augustine: The Bond of Friendship," *Studia Patristica* 33 (1996): 94–99; here, 95. I am grateful to Jeremy Bergstrom for this reference.

11. Augustine, *Confessions*, trans. Henry Chadwick (Oxford: Oxford University Press, 1991).

12. Kyle Harper, *From Shame to Sin: The Christian Transformation of Sexual Morality in Late Antiquity* (Cambridge, MA: Harvard University Press, 2013).

13. "Christian [sexual] austerity represented a radical freedom from the demands of the world" (Harper, *From Shame to Sin*, 213). For more on this, see esp. 82–99 and chap. 4.

14. Harrison, "Marriage and Monasticism in St. Augustine," 97. I am grateful to both Jeremy Bergstrom and Stephen Hildebrand, who, at different times, helped me understand the broader point of this section.

15. "Patebunt etiam cogitations nostrae invicem nobis" (Augustine, *City of God* XXII.29). I am grateful to Eric Gregory for this reference and its translation.

Chapter 9 Is There Friendship in the Trinity?

1. All quotations in this section are from Augustine, *On the Trinity* 6.5.7, as translated in the Nicene and Post-Nicene Fathers first series, vol. 3, found online at https://www.ccel.org/ccel/schaff/npnf103.html (among other places).

2. "Augustine, in describing the relation between the three persons of the Trinity, considers *amicitia* [friendship] to be the most appropriate word to express this relation." Caroline White, *Christian Friendship in the Fourth Century* (Cambridge: Cambridge University Press, 1992), 54.

Chapter 10 Examples of Friendship

1. In the supplementary material on the DVD, Bill Murray says, rather haltingly, that there is a standard romantic story line that we are familiar with, and at a certain point it goes one way or the other. But both ways, he says, are "incorrect for me"; they are "almost not true." This is because at the point where people decide to consummate an affair, they typically belittle their other lives as a way of justifying to themselves and to the other person the choice they are making. Murray says he's "very proud" of this scene; "it's one of the nicest scenes I've ever made." From "A Conversation with Bill Murray and Sofia Coppola," *Lost in Translation*, directed by Sofia Coppola (Los Angeles: Universal Studios, 2003), DVD.

2. J. K. Rowling, *Harry Potter and the Order of the Phoenix* (New York: Scholastic, 2003), 843–44.

3. Mark Twain, *The Adventures of Huckleberry Finn*, in *Mississippi Writings*, The Library of America (New York: Literary Classics of the United States, 1982), 834–35.

4. Twain, *Adventures of Huckleberry Finn*, 841.

5. Here I extend language used by Oliver O'Donovan to unpack friendliness. "In being friendly . . . we say, in effect, 'I am not your friend, nor you mine, nor in this life are we ever likely to become friends; yet in God's eternity, and even in this life if it should so transpire, a friendship between us will be no bad thing.'" Oliver O'Donovan, *Entering into Rest*, vol. 3 of *Ethics as Theology* (Grand Rapids: Eerdmans, 2017), 145.

6. O'Donovan, *Entering into Rest*, 136–39.

7. Francisco de Vitoria, "On the American Indians" (*De Indis*), in *Vitoria: Political Writings*, ed. Anthony Pagden and Jeremy Lawrance (Cambridge: Cambridge University Press, 1991), 231–92.

8. See C. S. Lewis, *Perelandra* (New York: Macmillan, 1944). Oliver O'Donovan has praise for the "serious philosophical intent" of the first volume of the trilogy, *Out of the Silent Planet*: "If we imagine a species wholly different from us biologically . . . and possessing more or less comparable powers of reason, with which we could communicate fully and at will by speech . . . we should simply conclude that the 'kind' laying claim upon us was constituted not by one biological species alone but by an intercommunicating *ensemble* of two or more species." Which is to say, our "neighbor" in that case would not have to be human. Oliver O'Donovan, *Finding and Seeking*, vol. 2 of *Ethics as Theology* (Grand Rapids: Eerdmans, 2014), 64.

9. Kazuo Ishiguro, *Never Let Me Go* (New York: Knopf, 2005).

10. The title of the novel, *You Shall Know Them*, evokes the saying of Jesus in the Sermon on the Mount: "Ye shall know them by their fruits" (Matt. 7:16). Vercors is identified by name, and his Resistance writing is characterized on the dust jacket as quoted above: Vercors, *You Shall Know Them*, trans. Rita Barisse (Boston: Little, Brown, 1953).

11. Mary Doria Russell, *The Sparrow* (New York: Fawcett Columbine/Ballantine, 1996); see also the sequel, *Children of God* (New York: Fawcett/Random House, 1998). I was introduced to *The Sparrow* by the wife of one of my oldest friends, and a few years later, when I praised it, a seminary student gave me the sequel. Friendship is something that comes to us in layers upon layers.

12. Ernest Cline, *Ready Player One* (New York: Crown Publishers, 2011). I was introduced to this book by the son of a priest—another instance of the human desire to deepen and expand friendship.

Chapter 11 All Together Now

1. Robert W. Jenson, *Song of Songs* (Louisville: John Knox Press, 2005).

2. One may read the opening chapters of Job as a sort of reverse mirror of the opening chapters of Genesis, with the difference that Job, unlike Adam, does not fall. So the blessing of Genesis 1 (be fruitful and multiply) is fulfilled in Job's large family and estate. Job has dominion over his animals; his children feast as people who do not experience the world as one of work and toil; there is even a hint of Sabbath observance in the timing of Job's intercessions in 1:5. His world collapses in an order suggested by Genesis 1–2: first the animals die, then the children. Satan asks if he can afflict Job's bone and flesh (Job 2:5); Adam recognized Eve as bone of his bone and flesh of his flesh. At 2:9, Job's wife appears, and she tempts Job to curse God. Michael Legaspi says that the significance of all this lies in Job being an exemplar of wisdom: he fears the Lord; he eschews evil; he is blameless and upright. Most of all, he speaks wisely. When he learns of the deaths of his animals, servants, and children, he speaks of nakedness: "Naked came I out of my mother's womb, and naked shall I return thither" (1:21). Legaspi connects this introduction of "nakedness" also with Genesis. Job, who obviously will not return to his mother's womb naked, is referring to the earth and thus echoing (embracing for himself) the words of the Lord spoken to Adam, who "knew" he was naked (vulnerable, mortal): "Dust thou art, and unto dust shalt thou return" (Gen. 3:19). Legaspi's book is extraordinarily rich throughout. For the contents of this note, see Michael C. Legaspi, *Wisdom in Classical and Biblical Tradition* (New York: Oxford University Press, 2018), 87–91.

3. See, for an accessible example, Robert W. Jenson, *A Theology in Outline: Can These Bones Live?*, ed. Adam Eitel (New York: Oxford University Press, 2016), chap. 4.

Postscript

1. Oliver O'Donovan, *Entering into Rest*, vol. 3 of *Ethics as Theology* (Grand Rapids: Eerdmans, 2017), 145.

2. Marilynne Robinson, *Gilead* (New York: Farrar, Straus and Giroux, 2004), 132–33.

Scripture Index

Subject Index

Abram/Abraham, 51–52, 54–56, 59–60, 73, 144
Adventures of Huckleberry Finn, The (Mark Twain), 133–34
Aelred, 82, 95, 99, 121, 164n6
  fall from friendship, 88–90
  God is friendship, 117–18
  real friendship is spiritual, 90–92
  Spiritual Friendship (Hill), 83–92
agape, 75, 79, 86
Alter, Robert, 162n2
amicitia, 43, 79, 85–86, 118, 121, 165n2. See also *De Amicitia*
Aquinas, 79–82, 121, 164n4
  on creation and beginning, 30
Aristotle, 14–27, 29, 32–34, 37, 59, 72, 90, 107
  Eudemian Ethics, 16–26, 159n1 (chap. 2), 160n2 (chap. 2)
  friendship as pleasantest thing, 20, 25, 91, 126, 132
  friendship as point of human life, 15–16, 22–26
  real friendship, 19–22
  theological questions, 22–27
Augustine, 76–79, 83, 110
  death of a friend, 77–78
  friendship in the Trinity, 119–121, 165n2

marriage oriented to friendship, 96–97, 109, 113–14
author vis-à-vis characters, 54–56, 146–47

Bachelor, The, and *The Bachelorette* (television series), 101
beauty, 25, 39–40, 108, 144, 155
Bennett, Jana Marguerite, 164n6
Book of Common Prayer, 4, 105–6, 157, 165n7
Brown, Raymond E., 163n11 (chap. 6)

Call Me by Your Name (film), 165n8
caritas, 79, 86, 90–91, 118, 121
Carmichael, E. D. H., 163n2
cats, 30, 32, 87
celibacy, 93–107. *See also* sex
child of God, 75–76, 121–23
Cicero, 41, 78, 83–84, 86, 91, 107
  Laelius de Amicitia, 41–47
clones, friendship of and with, 137–39
Colón, Christine A., 164n6
Comforters, The (Muriel Spark), 55–57
creation, 29–33, 51, 160n1
  creator cannot love, 54–56

Dante
  Paradiso, 107

171